THREE KIWI TALES

MORE FABULOUS FIX-IT STORIES FROM WILDBASE HOSPITAL

JANET HUNT

MASSEY UNIVERSITY PRESS

This is a companion book to *How to Mend a Kea + Other Fabulous Fix-it Tales from Wildbase Hospital*

Key: b = bottom; t = top
Cover: Koa, a Haast tokoeka O.N.E. chick, West Coast Wildlife Centre/Kimberley Revelly
Rod Morris: p.9–11, p.12. Kerry Oates: p.12, p.13t
Rainbow Springs/Emma Bean: p.13b, p.15, p.16t, p.17, p.18, p.38
Manawatu Evening Standard/Stuff: p37. Sian Reynolds: p.22, p.23
All others are either from Wildbase Hospital or by the author

First published in 2019 by Massey University Press
Private Bag 102904, North Shore Mail Centre, Auckland 0745, New Zealand
www.masseypress.ac.nz

Design by Janet Hunt

A catalogue record for this book is available from the National Library of New Zealand

Printed and bound in China by 1010 Printing International Ltd
ISBN: 978-0-9951001-4-5

CONTENTS

NGĀ MIHI

JUST AS IT IS in the endless task of caring for wildlife, writing a book is a team effort. *Three Kiwi Tales* would not have happened without the contributions of many people.

Top of the list are Pauline Nijman, Wildbase Hospital and Recovery Supervisor, and Emma Bean, Husbandry Manager at the National Kiwi Hatchery Aotearoa at Rainbow Springs in Rotorua. Pauline and Emma not only star in the stories, they have also been unstinting with time and assistance. What amazing, knowledgeable, caring, cheerful people they are. I'm in awe of their hard work on behalf of our endangered kiwi. Thank you so much, Pauline and Emma!

Many others have answered queries no matter how small, and helped with stories, contacts and photographs. In no particular order, my huge appreciation and thanks to Kerry Oates, Jacinda Amey, Sian Reynolds, Kimberley Revelly, Sorrel Hoskin, Riki Dallas, Philip Marsh, George Gibbs, Jo Russell, Michelle Bird, Kevin Stokes and the Taranaki Kiwi Trust.

Special thanks also to Brett Gartrell, Megan Jolly and the rest of the team of veterinarians and technicians at Wildbase Hospital, who allowed me to peer over their shoulders, listen in at meetings and generally get in the way.

Thanks, too, to the MUP publishing team of Tracey Borgfeldt, Nicola Legat and Anna Bowbyes for their support and encouragement.

And, as ever, a big thank you to Peter Haines and my family, friends, neighbours and fellow Taranaki conservationists. This is where it all begins.

INTRODUCTION

THIS BOOK IS ABOUT three kiwi: little Latitude, lovely Raratoka and Piwi the pioneer. It's also about two worlds. The worlds are extreme opposites, but there are times when they meet and overlap.

The first is the world of kiwi. It's a night-time place of dark, leafiness, the forest floor, burrows, worms, grubs, spiders and insects. It's the seemingly simple world to which, over millions of years, its kiwi inhabitants have become superbly adapted. They spend their days holed up, sleeping underground, and their nights out, roaming and feeding in defined territories, often in pairs. It's a natural world, but make no mistake, it is under attack, threatened by habitat loss and by an army of introduced kiwi-killers such as stoats, rats, cats and dogs.

The human world of Wildbase Hospital at Massey University could scarcely be more different. It's a sophisticated, high-tech, daytime place, shiny-bright, white-and-light, full of astonishing machines such as X-ray (radiograph) and ultrasound scanners and all the analysers, instruments, tools and trappings of modern medicine. This world is populated by wildlife veterinarians, technicians, scientists, students, administrators and helpers.

Beyond those worlds but tying them together is a web of other humans. They come from the Department of Conservation, bird rescue centres, wildlife sanctuaries and kiwi hatcheries around the country. They monitor kiwi, gather eggs and chicks, check traplines, drive the birds to places of safety . . . and to Wildbase. For many, it's their job. Countless others are unpaid volunteers. They all do it because it's their passion.

They know that *every kiwi counts.*

THE NOT-BIRD BIRD

KIWI ARE SO VERY WEIRD that when a kiwi skin was taken to England in 1812, a lot of people thought it was a giant hoax. It was as if a prankster had glued a whole lot of parts together for a laugh. After all, it didn't have much in the way of wings, it didn't have tail feathers, it had fluff instead of flight feathers, a ridiculously long bill, and legs like small tree trunks. *How could it be a bird?* Some thought it was a species of penguin; others thought it was a kind of dodo, a large, flightless, trusting bird that once lived on the island of Mauritius but was last seen in 1662.

The kiwi is a bird, all right, but it is indeed the strangest in the world. It's not surprising that it seemed like a joke.

THE HIHI, A TYPICAL BIRD

HIHI ARE DIURNAL. THEY LIVE IN THE DAY AND ARE CREATURES OF THE AIR AND SKY. ALMOST EVERYTHING ABOUT THEM EXISTS BECAUSE THEY HAVE EVOLVED FOR FLIGHT.

THEY LAY MANY EGGS, HAVE HELPLESS CHICKS THAT MUST BE FED BY THEIR PARENTS, AND LIVE IN HIGH PLACES WHERE THEY NEST AND ROOST. THEY HAVE:

- KEEN EYESIGHT
- A RUBBISH SENSE OF SMELL
- POOR HEARING
- NOSTRILS AT THE TOP OF THEIR BILLS
- FLIGHT FEATHERS
- WINGS AND A TAIL
- A KEEL ON THE BREASTBONE, WHERE THEIR WINGS ARE ATTACHED
- LIGHT, HOLLOW BONES
- THIN, DELICATE SKIN
- A BODY TEMPERATURE OF 39–42°C
- AND ONE OVARY.

- KIWI ARE RATITES, LIKE OSTRICHES AND EMUS. THEY DON'T HAVE WINGS, SO THEY HAVE NO KEEL FOR FLIGHT MUSCLES. INSTEAD, THEY HAVE A FLAT BREASTBONE AND WEAK CHEST MUSCLES. THAT'S WHY DOGS ARE SUCH A THREAT — ONE BITE CAN INSTANTLY KILL A KIWI
- AT 38°C, A KIWI'S BODY TEMPERATURE IS MORE LIKE A MAMMAL'S THAN A BIRD'S (HUMANS = 37°C)
- KIWI HAVE TWO OVARIES AND LAY MASSIVE EGGS
- KIWI CHICKS ARE PRECOCIAL — THEY ARE PERFECTLY FORMED COPIES OF ADULT KIWI FROM THE MOMENT THEY HATCH

SCIENTISTS DEVELOP NEW THEORIES all the time. Right now, they believe that prehistoric ancestors of kiwi very likely flew to New Zealand so long ago that we cannot imagine it — between 60,000,000 and 80,000,000 years ago. Those ancestor-kiwi would have had wings, feathers and a tail, and who knows what colour they were, or what size and shape their legs and bill were? What did they eat? We'll never know for sure, because there is no fossil evidence from way back then to tell us.

In the millions of years that followed, the ancestor-kiwi and all the plants, birds and other living creatures had New Zealand to themselves. Their world was a giant time capsule, a kingdom of birds that remained largely unchanged as the rest of the globe moved on. It was unlike any other place on Earth.

Safe on their islands, the ancestor-kiwi slowly changed, and changed again, until they became the species we know today.

LIKE MANY OTHER NEW ZEALAND BIRDS, ancestor-kiwi lost the power of flight. Flying requires immense amounts of energy to get off the ground and stay there. That is why flying birds are so streamlined, with no unnecessary weighty parts. But if there is no need to fly . . . you don't.

Kiwi wings became smaller until all that remained was a tiny limb, like a bent matchstick with a claw on the end. *No use at all!*

Kiwi feathers became dull, for better camouflage in the forest, and because they were not needed for flight, the feathers lost their rigid structures and became soft and hair-like instead, for warmth.

And as they traded in their wings, kiwi developed heavy bones and great strong legs for getting around, for running, kicking, digging and scratching.

They became nocturnal, going out at night and sleeping through the day. That way they could avoid hunting birds such as the terrifying Haast's eagle and birds of prey like harrier hawks and falcons. Night-time was also better for finding food. Kiwi kai — beetles, moths, wētā, cockroaches, millipedes, worms and other invertebrates, including those that live underground — is more plentiful and easier to catch after dark.

Adjusting to night living meant that kiwi eyes grew smaller and weaker at the same time as their hearing and senses of smell and touch grew stronger.

Altogether, kiwi became more like a mammal than a bird . . . and that is a great irony, because the greatest threats to kiwi are from mammals!

THE FIRST MAMMALS to arrive in New Zealand were the Polynesian voyagers and settlers who hauled their waka up the beaches around 800 years ago, along with their smaller companions, kiore (bush rats) and kurī (dogs).

The arrival of this trio was as much a disaster for native wildlife as if a giant meteor had exploded in the skies over the land. The humans hunted birds for food and feathers, and burned their living places, while kiore and kurī chomped their way into the forests.

One way or another, over the next centuries 34 bird species became extinct along with numerous amphibians, fish, reptiles, one bat and countless invertebrates.

Worse followed. About 500 years later, when new settlers

arrived from Europe, they transformed the land, felling trees to make farms, draining wetlands, and building towns, roads and cities. They also hunted and fished.

And they brought with them a whole new mob of invaders: cats, dogs, rabbits, possums, stoats, weasels, ferrets, mice, two more kinds of rat, hedgehogs, pigs, goats, deer, sheep and cows, and more. Some of those animals eat the same food as native wildlife, and others eat the wildlife itself.

New Zealand birds and other creatures were helpless, especially against the fiercer members of that gang. Like kiwi, many birds nest on or near the ground, making it easy for hunters like dogs, cats, possums, stoats and rats to kill nesting adults, steal and devour eggs, and slaughter chicks. Kiwi's strong musky smell is like an flashing neon advertisement to mammals, with their sensitive noses — *Look! Over here! Here I am!*

Another 16 species of bird disappeared forever.

Shriek! This young kiwi had no chance against the stoat.

THE KIWI WHO'S WHO

THERE ARE FIVE KIWI SPECIES in Aotearoa New Zealand. They belong to the genus *Apteryx,* which is a Latin word for 'no wing', because when they were named in London in 1812 by Dr George Shaw, he hadn't noticed their tiny wings. The wings appear to be of no use at all, but sometimes, when the birds sleep, they tuck their long bill comically under the barely existent limb.

Perhaps they dream of times long ago when they had larger wings and took to the air to soar effortlessly over ocean and forest . . .

BROWN KIWI *Apteryx mantelli*

Brown kiwi occur naturally in the wild in the North Island. Their slightly reddish feathers have dark edges, making them look streaked with brown and black. There are four distinct groups, each a little different genetically: the Coromandel brown kiwi, the Northland brown kiwi, the eastern brown kiwi and the western brown kiwi.

Length: 40 cm **Weight**: 2.2 kg (male), 2.8 kg (female)

Threat level: At risk–declining

GREAT SPOTTED KIWI / ROROA *Apteryx haastii*

As the 'great' in their English name tells us, great spotted kiwi, or roroa, are the giants of the kiwi world; they have pearl-grey feathers flecked with bands of darker grey. They live in the hills and mountain ranges, forests and tussock grasslands of the upper South Island.

Length: 50 cm **Weight**: 2.6 kg (male), 3.3 kg (female)

Threat level: Threatened–nationally vulnerable

LITTLE SPOTTED KIWI / KIWI PUKUPUKU *Apteryx owenii*

Little spotted is clearly the tiniest kiwi species. Their feathers are soft brownish-grey over white, which makes them seem spotted. They have whitish legs and long pale bills. They were once widespread throughout the country, but are now extinct in the wild on the mainland, surviving only on offshore islands and in sanctuaries.

Length: 30 cm **Weight**: 1.1 kg (male), 1.3 kg (female)

Threat level: At risk–recovering

ŌKĀRITO BROWN KIWI / ROWI *Apteryx rowi*

Rowi are the rarest of all kiwi species, numbering about 500. They are found in the Ōkārito and south Westland forests. They are similar in size to brown kiwi but have soft, greyish feathers streaked with brown and black, and sometimes white around their heads. Unlike other kiwi species, they have strong family ties, with young kiwi sometimes remaining in the family group for years.

Length: 40 cm **Weight**: 1.9 kg (male), 2.6 kg (female)

Threat level: Threatened–nationally vulnerable

TOKOEKA / SOUTHERN BROWN KIWI *Apteryx australis*

Ngāi Tahu's name for this large southern brown kiwi is 'tokoeka', which translates as 'weka with a walking stick'. *Totally right!* That's exactly how they appear as they walk along tapping their bills on the ground.

Tokoeka are similar to Ōkārito rowi. They have reddish-dark brown soft feathers streaked with brown and black, a long, pale bill, and short, whitish legs and toes.

There are three sub-groups. The first, Rakiura/Stewart Island tokoeka (threatened–nationally critical) are unusual because they sometimes go beachcombing in daylight, looking in seaweed for invertebrates to eat.

The other two sub-groups, Fiordland tokoeka (threatened–nationally vulnerable) and the rare Haast tokoeka (threatened–nationally critical), like to live in the mountains, which makes them tricky to find and care for.

Length: 45 cm **Weight**: 2.4 kg (male), 3.1 kg (female)

The length measurement is for females, which are larger than their mates, and is taken from bill to bottom.

Read more and see some great photos at NZ Birds online, kiwisforkiwi or the Department of Conservation websites.

See page 46 for how to read threat levels.

Three tokoeka sub-groups. [1] Rakiura/Stewart Island tokoeka, [2] Fiordland tokoeka and [3] a seven-month-old Haast tokoeka.

LATITUDE'S TALE

THEY CALLED HIM LATITUDE . . . but not at first. In the beginning, he was simply an egg named 'Mn.Arp5'. Even then, he was something out of the ordinary.

Mn.Arp5 came from Manunui Forest, in the rugged hill country halfway between Tongariro National Park and the Whanganui River. His father was Arapeta, a western brown kiwi. Mn.Arp5's mother was a very large brown kiwi named Mrs Peta.

[1] This is Arapeta's nest. Can you spot Mn.Arp5?

[2] Delia, one of Kerry's helpers, holds Arapeta while Kerry retrieves Mn.Arp5.

IT WAS FRIDAY afternoon, 2 November 2018. Manunui Project Manager Kerry Oates was in the forest doing his kiwi rounds. He had lifted an egg from Arapeta in October, so it was too soon to expect another. Instead, he was giving Arapeta a six-monthly health check and, at the same time, was going to switch the kiwi's radio transmitter to a new one and put it on his other leg.

It's Mrs Peta's job to lay eggs — two, sometimes three, clutches, or times, a year. Mostly she lays two eggs in each, but they are so huge — six times larger than you might expect, taking up 20 per cent of her body weight — that she lays them about two weeks apart. It takes a week for her to form an egg. It's a massive task.

After that, she is free to go and the job passes to Arapeta. He develops a brood patch on his tummy, which has no feathers, and blood vessels close to the skin, to keep the eggs warm. As the eggs grow older, he stays with them more and more, sitting on them and turning them, keeping them toasty and safe.

The transmitter on Arapeta's leg tells Kerry what the kiwi is up to. When there are no eggs, he spends most of the night outside. The transmitter detects that he is on the move and sends the information to Kerry's antenna.

But if Arapeta is in the nest on an egg (or eggs, if there is a second one), the transmitter switches to incubation mode and tells Kerry that, too.

Not this time!

There was only one egg and, because it was not very old, Arapeta was out of the nest a lot of the time. The transmitter didn't signal that the egg was there.

Imagine Kerry's astonishment when he lifted the kiwi from his burrow and saw the large, pearly-white shape partly buried under leaves and moss in the bottom of the nest.

It's not usual to take newly laid eggs, but once he had disturbed Arapeta, Kerry had no choice — *if in doubt, bring it out* is the motto. Whatever Kerry did, Arapeta would have run away and not come back. The egg would have died.

Kerry didn't have his egg-gathering box with him. He candled the egg, which means he shone his torch through its thin shell so he could see inside. There was a small air cell at one end. It was important to know its location because the air cell must be upward when an egg is carried. He drew on the shell in pencil, marking the top of the egg and writing its name.

He tucked the egg into a fleece and carried it back to his ute. Then he wrapped it in a towel and placed it cross-wise in the space between the front seats. Off he went, trying his best not to shake or damage the egg.

Three and a half hours later, Kerry handed Mn.Arp5 over to Emma Bean. Emma is the Husbandry Manager at the National Kiwi Hatchery Aotearoa at Rainbow Springs in Rotorua. Mn.Arp5 weighed 450.3 grams and was 124.9 millimetres long by 80.5 millimetres wide.

The egg was dirty and it was cracked at one end.

[1] A helper holds a parka so Kerry is in darkness while he candles the egg.

[2] In safe hands! Emma from the National Kiwi Hatchery cradles a young brown kiwi.

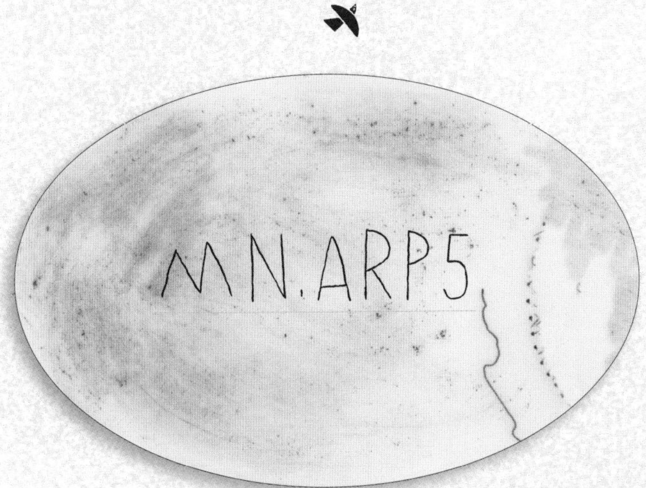

OPERATION NEST EGG

[1] On the outside, there's a delicate calcium carbonate shell with tiny pores that allow the egg to 'breathe': oxygen enters and water vapour and carbon dioxide leaves. Just inside the shell, there are two semi-transparent protein membranes, like very thin skin, that defend the egg from bacteria.

[2] The embryo. It starts as a tiny group of cells that you can hardly see and grows larger as organs form and it becomes more like a chick. By the time it hatches, it fills the whole egg.

[3] A special temporary membrane called the CAM or chorioallantoic membrane. The CAM has a network of veins that carry oxygen, food and waste to and from the growing embryo. It's like the placenta in mammals.

[4] The air cell (AC) at one end is a space between the outer membrane and the inner membrane. It's the gap at the blunt end of a boiled chicken egg when you peel it. The air cell provides oxygen to the chick just before it hatches, once the veins inside the CAM can no longer get enough oxygen through the pores of the shell. The AC enlarges as the egg gets older, whether there is an embryo or not, and is a sign of the age of the egg — that's why you can do a float test with supermarket eggs to find out how old they are! By hatching day, the AC occupies almost one third of the egg.

[5] Inside there is a large amount of yolk in a sac. It feeds the embryo as it grows and after it hatches. It fills up to 60 per cent of the space in the egg — much more than most birds. Emma says it's as if Kiwi Mum has packed lunch for her chick!

[6] The albumen, or egg white, contains proteins and water. It protects the yolk and provides additional nutrition.

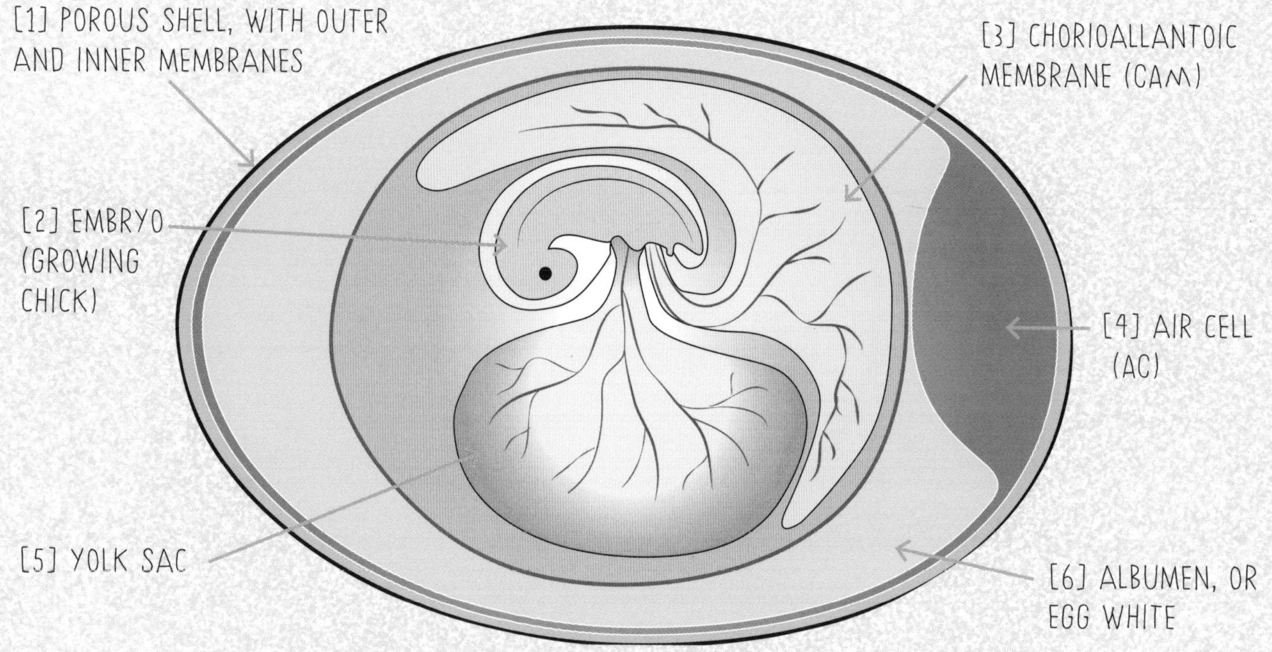

(THIS EGG IS ACTUAL SIZE, BUT THE PROPORTIONS INSIDE ALTER AS THE EGG GROWS)

ARAPETA AND HIS EGG, Mn.Arp5, were part of an an undertaking called Operation Nest Egg (O.N.E.).

Kiwi have lived in New Zealand forests for millions of years. They belong here and only here. There used to be hundreds of thousands of them, whistling and calling, snorting and pottering around doing kiwi things in the bush after dark.

But by the end of the twentieth century, that had changed. Because of habitat loss and because of predators, many forests were silent and empty while others had hardly any kiwi at all.

Not enough kiwi were growing up. *Ninety-five* young kiwi out of 100 eggs hatched were dying. No adults means no more eggs, no more chicks and no more kiwi. Without help, all kiwi were in danger of disappearing forever.

Dogs, cats, rats and pigs and other hunting mammals are all a threat to kiwi, but worst by far, and the trigger that tipped kiwi populations into a nose-dive, are stoats.

Stoats are mustelids, belonging to the same family as ferrets and weasels. They are superb hunters, they climb and they swim, they are fearless, they breed rapidly and they are everywhere.

And they are hungry: they eat eggs, they eat chicks, they eat young kiwi . . .

It was a crisis, but there was a glimmer of hope.

STOATS ARE RELUCTANT to attack large kiwi because of their mighty kicks and sharp claws. What was needed was some way to get young kiwi to the 'large kiwi' safe place, a bridge to carry them across that scary, dangerous time from egghood to adulthood. Operation Nest Egg was one very clever answer. It began in 1994.

Brown kiwi males sit on their eggs for an average of 78 days. In that time a fully formed Mini-Me kiwi chick develops, small but ready to look after itself from the moment it hatches. Operation Nest Egg succeeds because of this very thing: kiwi chicks know all they ever need to know right from the start. Kiwi parents *never* feed their chicks. Some species stay in family groups for a year or so, but not brown kiwi. After about five days getting up strength in the nest, the chick is off. *See you around, Dad!*

Under Operation Nest Egg, kiwi eggs are lifted from nests in the forest around day 60 and, like Mn.Arp5, they are taken to hatcheries around the country.

At the hatchery the egg is placed in an incubator. Great care is taken to ensure that the egg is warm and does not dry out. It is closely monitored and notes are kept to track its progress.

After the chick hatches, it is put into a specially warm, humidity-controlled box called a brooder, often with another chick for company.

Once it's feeding and growing as it should, it is moved to an outside area where people still keep an eye on it. Sometimes it goes to a kiwi crèche on an island or to another safe place such as a mainland sanctuary.

The little kiwi returns to the forest only when it is large enough to fend off stoats. By then it weighs over one kilogram and is usually over six months old.

It's been in the forest before — but at that time it was just an egg!

Welcome home, little kiwi.

MN.ARP5 WAS SO NEW when Kerry found it that, apart from the air cell, there was no sign of life. Emma guessed that the egg was about nine days old. *It might not make it.*

First, she mended the crack with nail varnish. Then she gently cleaned, weighed and measured Mn.Arp5, and placed it in an incubator. For 60 days the incubator kept the air humid and the egg warm. Mn.Arp5 was turned four times a day, first by hand and later in an automatic incubator. Emma and others in the team took turns to weigh and candle it twice a week.

By the end of December they could make out the outline of a small chick inside. When Emma whistled to the egg, it wobbled, jiggled and twitched as the chick responded. But it was not as lively as it should have been. They were concerned, so Emma sent the egg to the vet in Rotorua for an X-ray.

1

There was the problem! The chick was folded and jammed sideways across the egg instead of longways. That's when they named him Latitude, because 'latitude' is the word for the side-to-side measurement of something.

LATITUDE WAS STUCK! He had grown too big. His long kiwi bill was preventing him from turning his head. He was running low on oxygen and needed to make what is called an 'internal pip': he needed to break into the air cell — but he couldn't move.

Using the X-ray as a guide, Emma and the team tapped a tiny view hole into the shell, and then, ever so carefully, they tore another tiny hole in the membrane of the air cell near Latitude's nostrils. How handy that kiwi nostrils are at the tip of their bills! *Whew!* Latitude took his first breath.

Emma taped over the view hole and left him to carry on hatching. It took six more days.

First, because he had used up the oxygen in the air cell, Latitude cracked a small hole to the outside. This is called the 'external pip'. Now he could breathe comfortably.

Most birds have an egg-tooth that they use to chip through the shell, but a kiwi chick has to heave and thrust with its strong legs to break free. Latitude pushed and pushed.

It was exhausting and he took lots of rest stops, but at last there he was, a tiny, damp, sweaty kiwi. When his feathers dried, he was a ball of fluff with two bright eyes and a pretty pink bill.

It was Sunday, 6 January 2019.

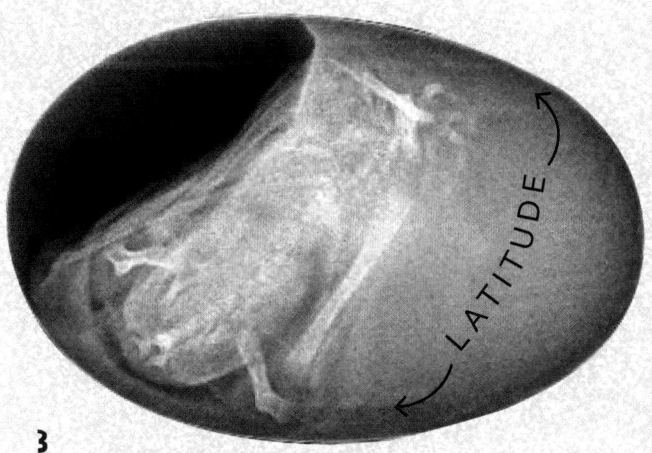

3

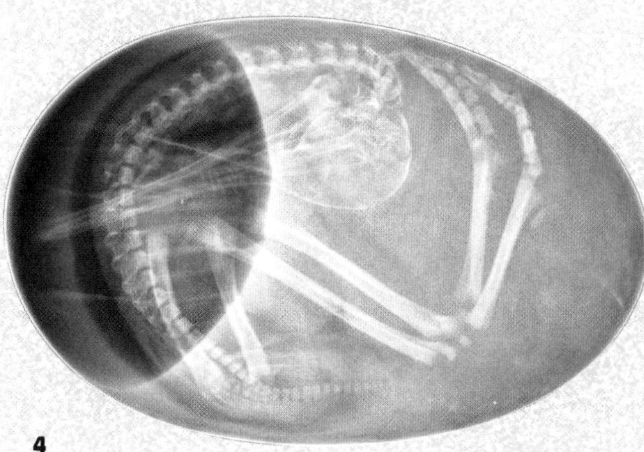

4

5

[1] Kiwi eggs, snug inside an incubator at National Kiwi Hatchery.

[2] The brooder room where Mn.Arp5 hatched.

[3] Latitude's X-ray. You may be able to make out his spine and bill.

[4] This is how an X-rayed egg *should* look. Can you see the bill and skull? You can also see the spine, the feet and legs and the air cell. It's getting tight in there, but it's still nowhere as cramped as it is inside Latitude's egg.

[5] It is such hard work! A newly hatched chick takes a rest.

BUT UH-OH, SOMETHING still was not right. Latitude's puku, his tummy, was so large and soft that he could not walk. His legs stuck out the side, and if he toppled over he couldn't get up again. Emma propped him up in a circle of towels.

What was his problem? While the embryo is growing in the egg, it is fed from a large yolk sac. Not long before hatching, the sac is drawn into the chick's body through its navel — which is just like a human belly-button. The yolk feeds the chick in its first days of life, while it recovers from hatching but before it starts eating with its bill.

Latitude's yolk sac was way bigger than it should be and it wasn't supplying him with food. He was given antibiotics in case it was infected, but they didn't help. After 11 days he was sliding downhill. His breath was wheezy, his bill was a dull colour and he didn't want to eat. He was struggling and likely to die. It was time to call for help!

There was a consultation with the local vet and a phone call to Palmerston North.

On 17 January, Latitude was flown in a box to Wildbase Hospital. He weighed 273 grams.

Latitude: just 5 days old and feeling poorly.

ALISON CLARKE WAS THE VET in charge of Latitude's treatment. In his first two days Latitude's blood was sampled and analysed and his poo was examined. He was chirpy but subdued, and he ate a teeny amount of minced ox-heart.

He was still on antibiotics. He was taken for ultrasound and X-rays. Just as everyone suspected, there was a large eggy shape pressing on his lungs and heart.

On the evening of Wednesday, 23 January, a tiny mask was placed over Latitude's bill and face and the isoflurane anaesthetic gas was turned on. He quickly became unconscious.

The feathers on his tummy were plucked and his skin was sterilised.

He was carried into surgery.

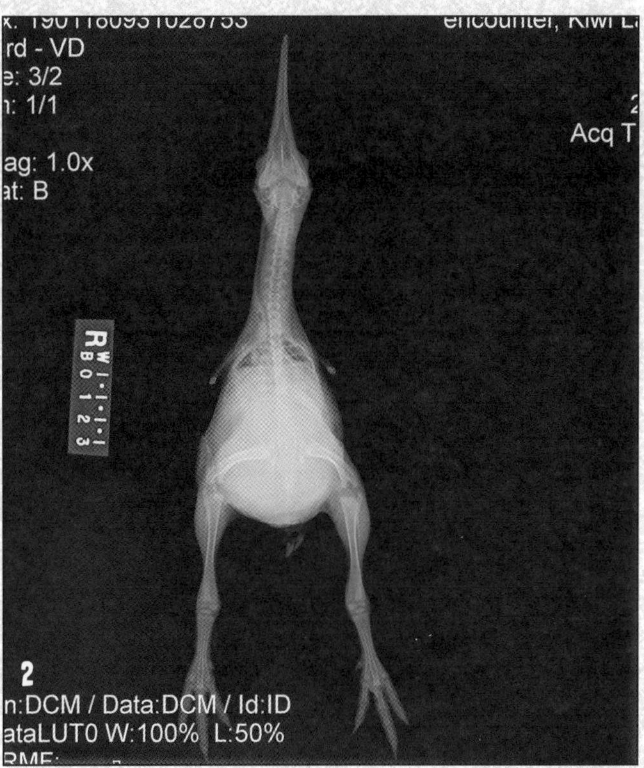

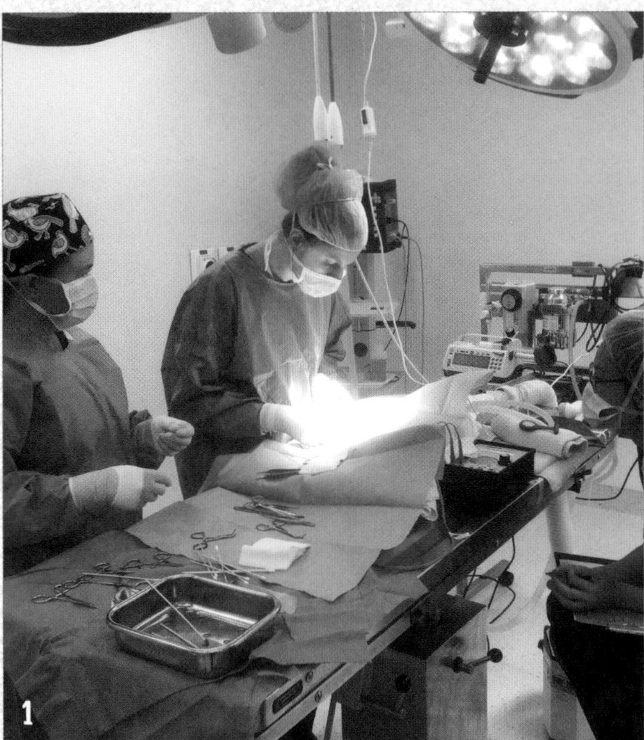

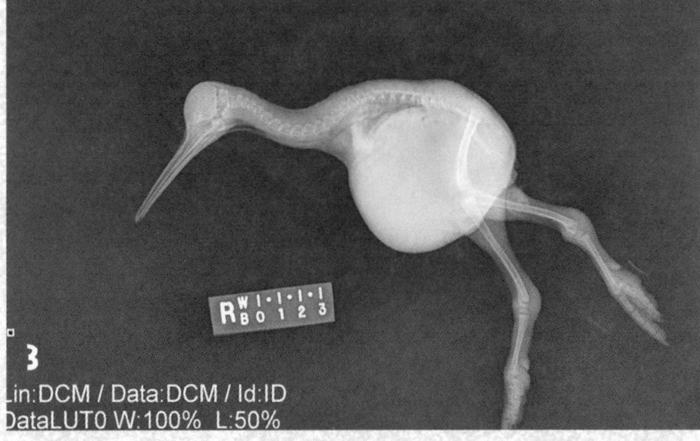

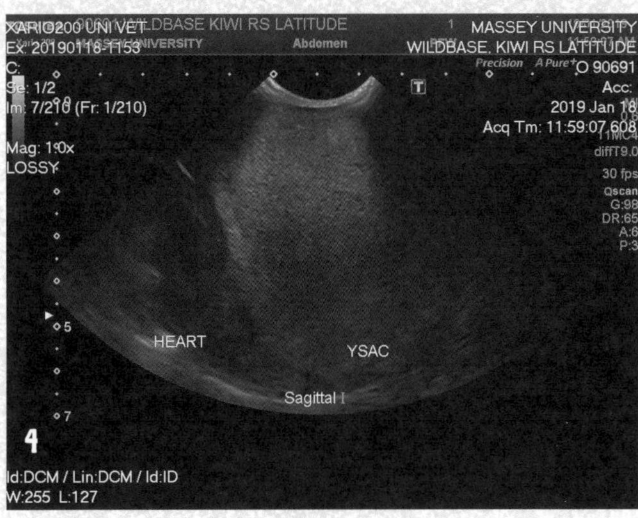

[1] Surgery is about to begin in the Wildbase operating theatre: Alison is assisted by Megan (left) and Christine (right).

[2] to **[4]** The Wildbase vets and technicians are experts at reading X-ray and ultrasound images. These were taken when Latitude was first examined. You can see his problem.

Alison sliced a circle around his navel, and a couple more incisions inside so she could see into his tummy. There was the troublesome yolk sac! She gently drew it out, tied and cut it off, and stitched him up again.

For a brief moment just after the sac was removed, Latitude's heart raced and thumped like a crazy-mad-running thing, but luckily it soon settled down.

The sac weighed 67.6 grams — a quarter of the chick's body weight! Back he went to his warm brooder to come round and sleep it off.

LATITUDE WAS SOON on the mend. His appetite returned. Within a week he was scoffing 30 grams of special kiwi kai and trashing his cage overnight just as a little wild kiwi should. *Great stuff!* He was looking marvellous, with a Harry Potter scar across his tummy.

His stitches were removed on 6 February, and he was discharged and driven back to the hatchery the next day. He weighed 284 grams, which is still not a lot — but at least it was all kiwi, and no longer included the great big sac of yolk.

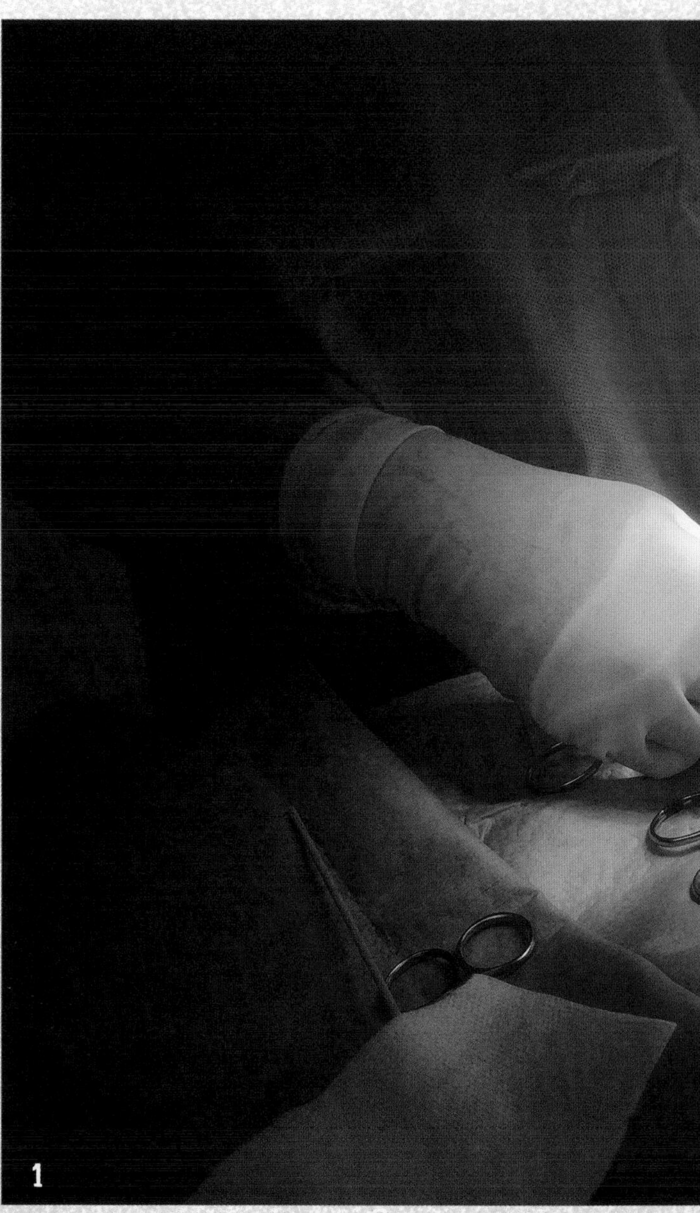

[1] Out it comes — surgery in the Wildbase operating theatre.
[2] The first incision into Latitude's plucked tummy.
[3] The tip of the yolk sac.
[4] and [5] The 67.6-gram yolk sac.

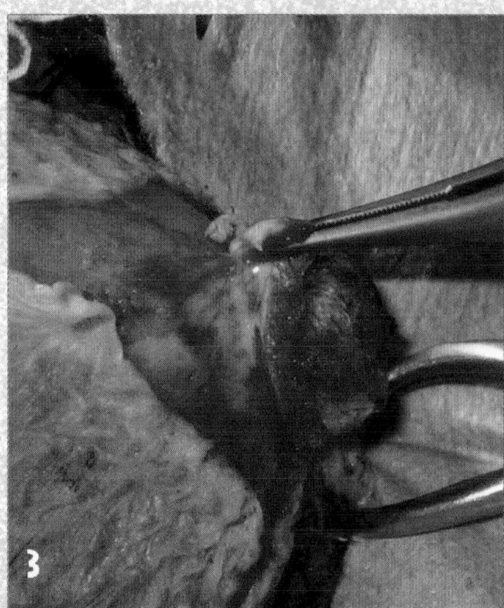

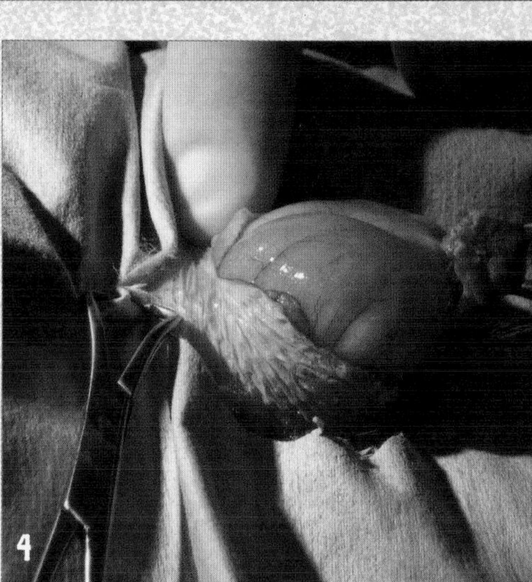

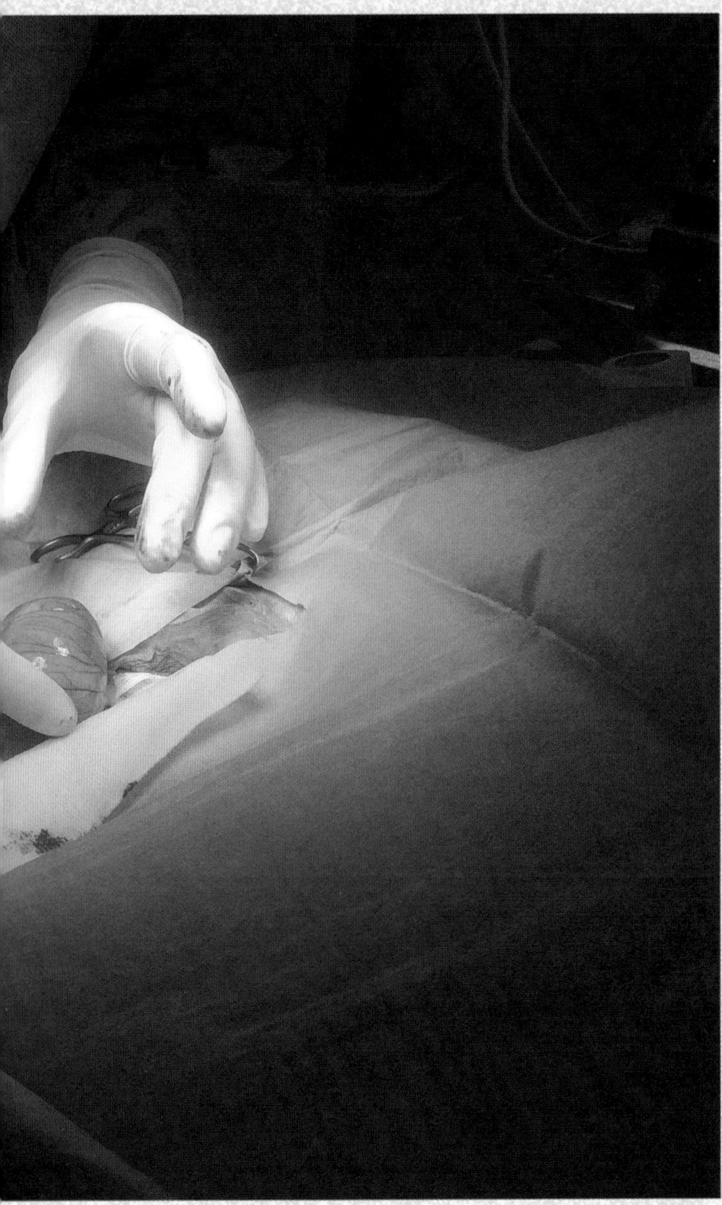

A FEW WEEKS LATER Emma wrote in his notes that Latitude was a 'beautiful, active chick'. *High five!*

He was microchipped and set free on Sanctuary Mountain Maungatautari. Sanctuary Mountain is fully fenced to keep predators out, so Latitude can keep doing his kiwi thing in complete safety and will grow into a fine adult.

He had a bumpy start to life, but he's on his way. *Brilliant!*

KIWI KAI

Latitude was eating a special 'kiwi maintenance diet' designed by Don Thomas at Massey University. Don wanted to be sure that kiwi chicks were getting all the nutrients they needed. In the wild they eat a lot of insects, earthworms and other grubs so they get plenty of variety. Don looked at the stomach contents of wild dead kiwi. He also looked at what was in the poo of wild kiwi. He made a mix that is mainly beef steak and ox-heart, but it also has fruit and veges, cat biscuits and a special vitamin and mineral mix. Just right.

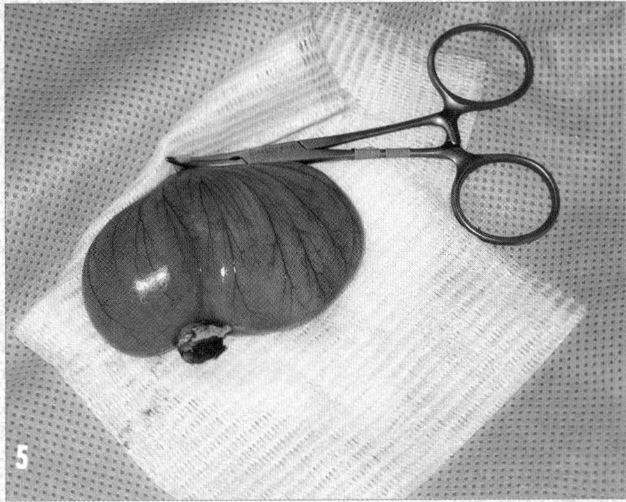

5

RARATOKA'S TALE

THE ISLAND is a grassy, shrubby, scrub-and-fern-covered 86-hectare chunk of rocky land at the western end of Foveaux Strait. It's cold, wild and windy, with sea-splashed, storm-lashed coasts. No people live here, but there's a working lighthouse and a couple of houses that once were home to lighthouse keepers and their families. The island belongs to Ōraka Aparima Rūnaka of Ngāi Tahu and is tapu. It has been a safe place for wildlife since 2006, when the last rats and mice were killed.

This tale begins with a kiwi that has been on the island since she was one year old. For the moment, let's call her by her Department of Conservation number, Tokoeka #36459. She's a Haast tokoeka, one of the rarest species of kiwi. Her father, Beeker, and her mother, Winglet, live near the bushline on a ridge about 500 metres up Mount Watney in the Haast Kiwi Sanctuary on the West Coast of the South Island. The sanctuary is in rugged, mountainous country with high peaks and deep valleys. It extends from the sea to sub-alpine grasslands.

Like Latitude, Tokoeka #36459 is an Operation Nest Egg chick. She hatches at Willowbank Wildlife Reserve in Christchurch in December 2007, and spends her first year on an island in Lake Te Anau. She is placed on the island in Foveaux Strait in 2009; she weighs 1.32 kilograms and is considered large enough to look after herself.

Hindley Ridge, high in the mountainous West Coast forests where Haast tokoeka hang out.

ON THE ISLAND our tokoeka becomes part of a kōhanga kiwi: 'kōhanga' means 'nursery' and that's what the island is — one great big kiwi nest! Kōhanga kiwi are an alternative, more natural and less expensive way of increasing kiwi numbers than Operation Nest Egg.

Altogether, 20 precisely selected young birds, including Tokoeka #36459, are placed on the island. None of the kiwi have transmitters, partly because they might snag in the muehlenbeckia vine that scrambles across much of the island, but mainly because no one ever intends to lift eggs and take them to a hatchery. The kiwi in the kōhanga are simply left to get on with living and breeding in safety.

Tokoeka #36459 is checked again later in 2009. She is much bigger and has a mate. Everything looks fine.

YEARS PASS. In 2016 a team of five Department of Conservation (DOC) staff with trained sniffer dogs visit the island, hoping to find many more kiwi than in 2009. They plan to take some back to the Haast sanctuary to add to the main population there. The work of the kōhanga will be done.

They set up headquarters in one of the houses.

The birds are hard to find. Dogs are normally superb at sniffing out kiwi, but not here, where thick grasses and undergrowth confuse the scent. A lot of the catching has to be at night. Apart from one day, the weather is terrible. They don't find any new young birds and only 14 of the older ones. Tokoeka #36459 is one. Her mate is another.

She is caught on a night when there are high winds and torrential rain. The DOC staff carry her back to the house. Under the lights of the porch, among the boots and wet-weather gear, they see immediately that something is not right. Tokoeka #36459's bill is thickened and yellowed towards the tip, not elegant, pale pink and tapering to a fine point as it should be. And even though she is tall for a kiwi, she is thin. She weighs just 2.3 kilograms, but should be nearer to 3 kilograms.

Along with all the other captured birds, Tokoeka #36459 is helicoptered off the island a week or so later. The rest, including her mate, are released in the Haast Kiwi Sanctuary. But there's only one place for Tokoeka #36459: Wildbase. She is flown by Air New Zealand from Invercargill to Palmerston North. It's a long trip.

And that's when she gets her new name. The staff at the hospital name her Raratoka, or 'south wind', after her island home.

One of the other captured tokoeka is released in the Haast Kiwi Sanctuary.

REMARKABILL

Step, tap, sniff-and-hold; step, tap, sniff-and-hold; step, tap, sniff-and-hold . . .

If you watch a kiwi looking for food, whether it is in the deepest, darkest night or brightest moonlight, it walks in rhythm, stepping and tapping its bill on the ground, like a blind person with a cane. It holds still for a second while it sniffs, feels and listens for vibrations that tell it of kiwi kai, *right there*, under the soil — perhaps a worm, a centipede, a millipede or a beetle?

A kiwi with a damaged or broken bill is in big trouble because . . .

A kiwi bill is a tool. It is hands, nose, mouth and even, to some extent, eyes, all in one.

A kiwi bill is a food-finder. Kiwi eyes are small and not much use, so their bills have turned into super-efficient feeling and smelling machines. All other birds have nostrils at the top of their bills next to their heads, but kiwi nostrils are at the very tip. The tip of the kiwi bill also has tiny, specialised pits packed with nerve endings that make it mega-sensitive to movement and vibration in the soil.

A kiwi bill is a digging tool. When a kiwi locates something, it probes to see what it is. It forces its bill deep into the soil. It levers back and forth and round and round until it has opened a hole up to 10 centimetres wide and 15 centimetres deep. Of course, those nostrils are easily blocked. *Snort! Snort!*

A kiwi bill is a mouth. Kiwi finds a worm and ever so gently tugs-and-pulls, tugs-and-pulls . . . *slurp!* Down the hatch. Just like eating spaghetti.

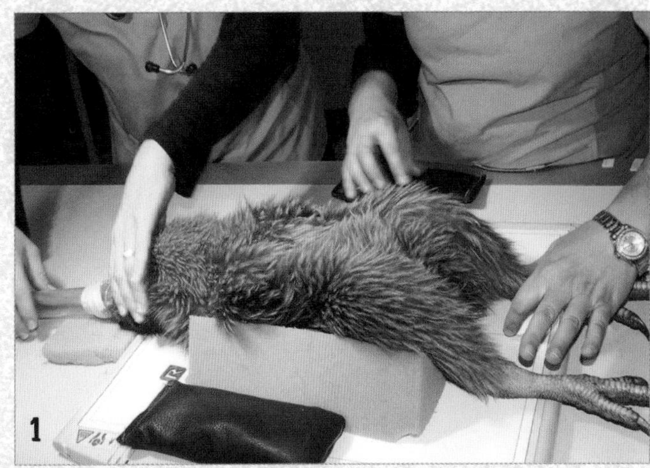

THE KIWI THAT EMERGES from the travelling crate is thin and has sore, reddened legs from sitting, but it's the bill that catches veterinarian Megan Jolly's eye. It's scabby and is wider than it should be.

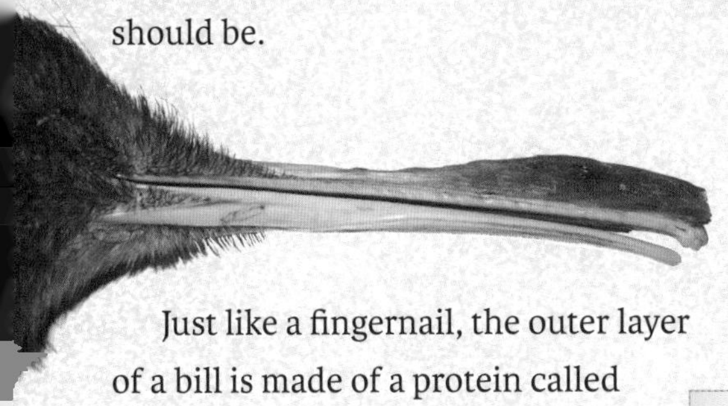

Just like a fingernail, the outer layer of a bill is made of a protein called keratin. And just like a fingernail, the keratin layer grows all the time. It takes constant digging and poking in the soil to keep it worn down and trimmed.

But it's a vicious cycle! Once the bill starts to overgrow it hurts and is harder to use; not being used makes the keratin grow more, which makes it harder to use . . . and so it goes, getting worse all the time.

Because there are no rats and mice on Raratoka's island, the undergrowth is crawling with bugs of all shapes and sizes. Raratoka has probably survived by mainly eating insects on the surface and not using her bill to probe.

What has happened?

They soon find some of the answer.

[1] Raratoka is stretched out for an X-ray.

[2] 'Let's look at you.' Brett Gartrell, the senior veterinarian and Wildbase clinical director, holds Raratoka steady, soon after she arrives at the hospital.

ON 17 MAY, Raratoka is given what the team calls a 'work up' under general anaesthetic. She is examined from bill to bottom, a blood sample is taken for testing, and her whole body, including her bill and head, is X-rayed. Megan can just make out a tiny fracture in the maxilla, about 45 millimetres from the tip. It's not broken right through and is covered by the overgrowth. Is it healing? There's no way to tell. There's no sign of infection or inflammation.

Still under anaesthetic, Raratoka is taken to surgery and the overgrown keratin is *debrided* — it is cut, scraped and polished away.

There are lots of important nerve endings in the bill. It almost certainly will *really hurt*. The kiwi is given medication to dull the pain when she comes round, and antibiotics to prevent infection.

And it begins: the long, hard journey to recovery.

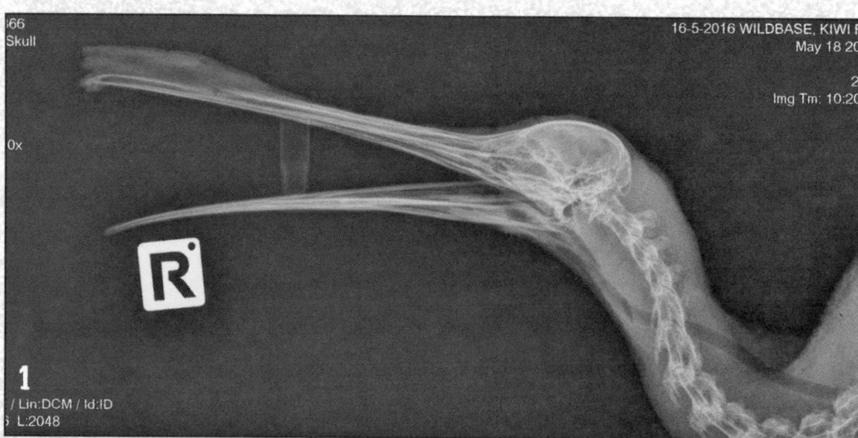

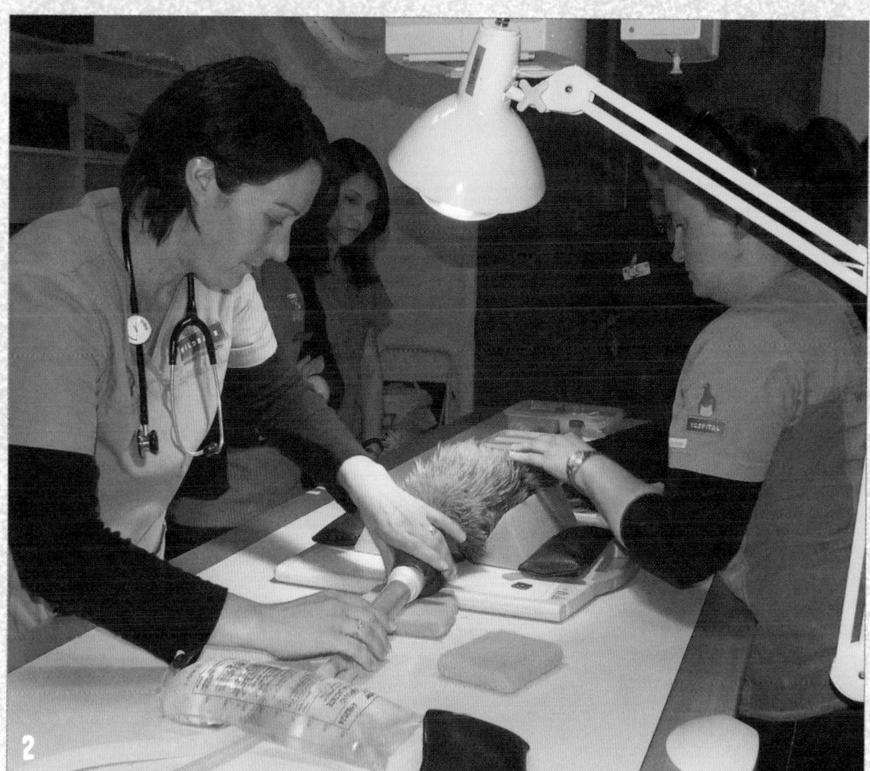

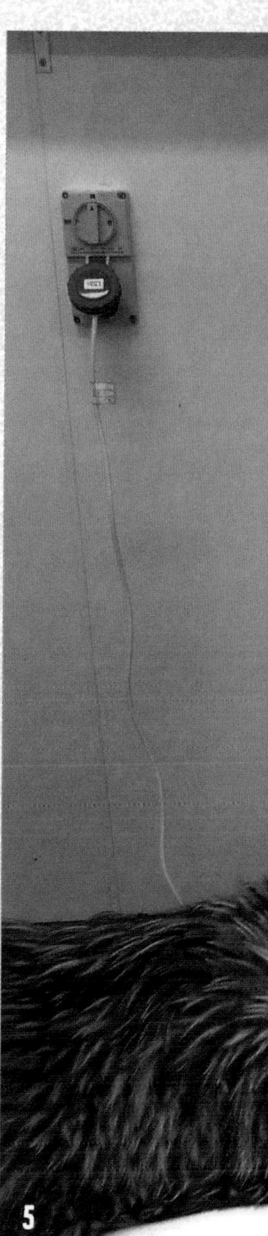

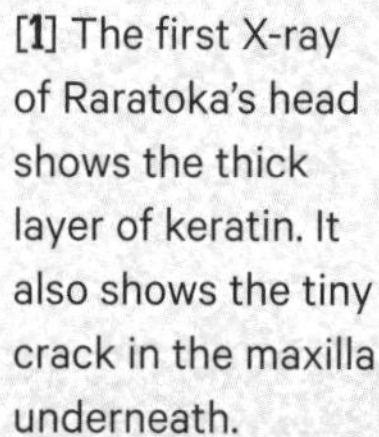

[1] The first X-ray of Raratoka's head shows the thick layer of keratin. It also shows the tiny crack in the maxilla underneath.

[2] Pauline (left) and Megan prepare Raratoka for X-rays while students observe.

[3] Raratoka, unconscious and ready for surgery.

[4] and [5] A tool called a dremel is used to buff off the old keratin.

[6] and [7] Megan also uses a scalpel to cut the keratin away.

3

DREMEL
MultiPro
10,000-37,000
OFF

4

Nervous System
Air Sacs/Infraorbital Sinus
FIRST AID
WILDBASE
MASSEY UNIVERSITY

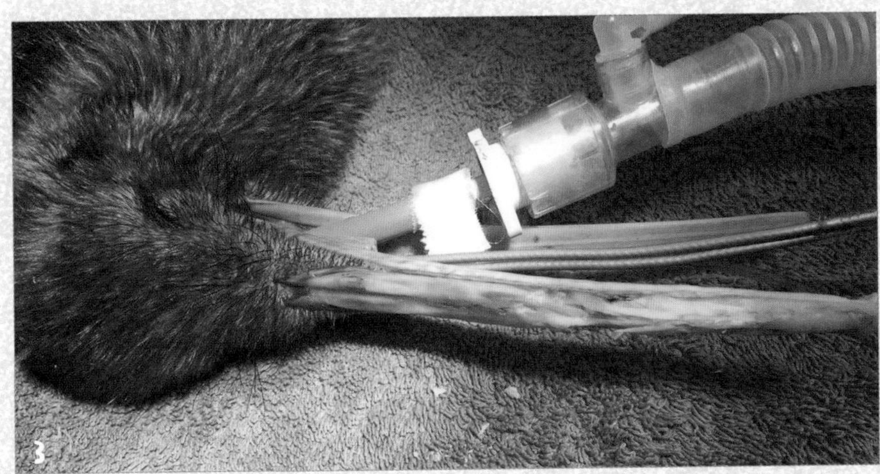

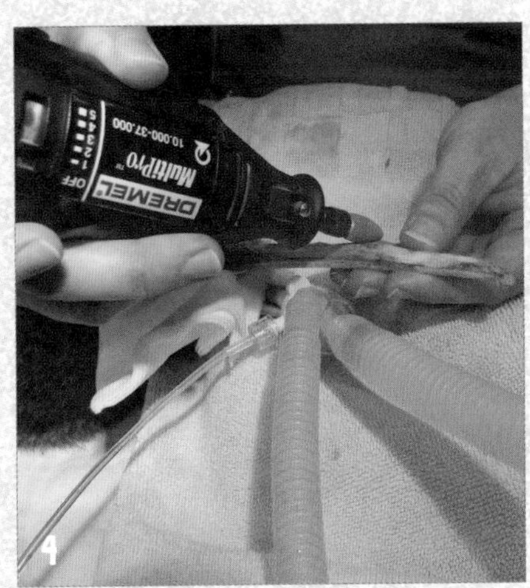

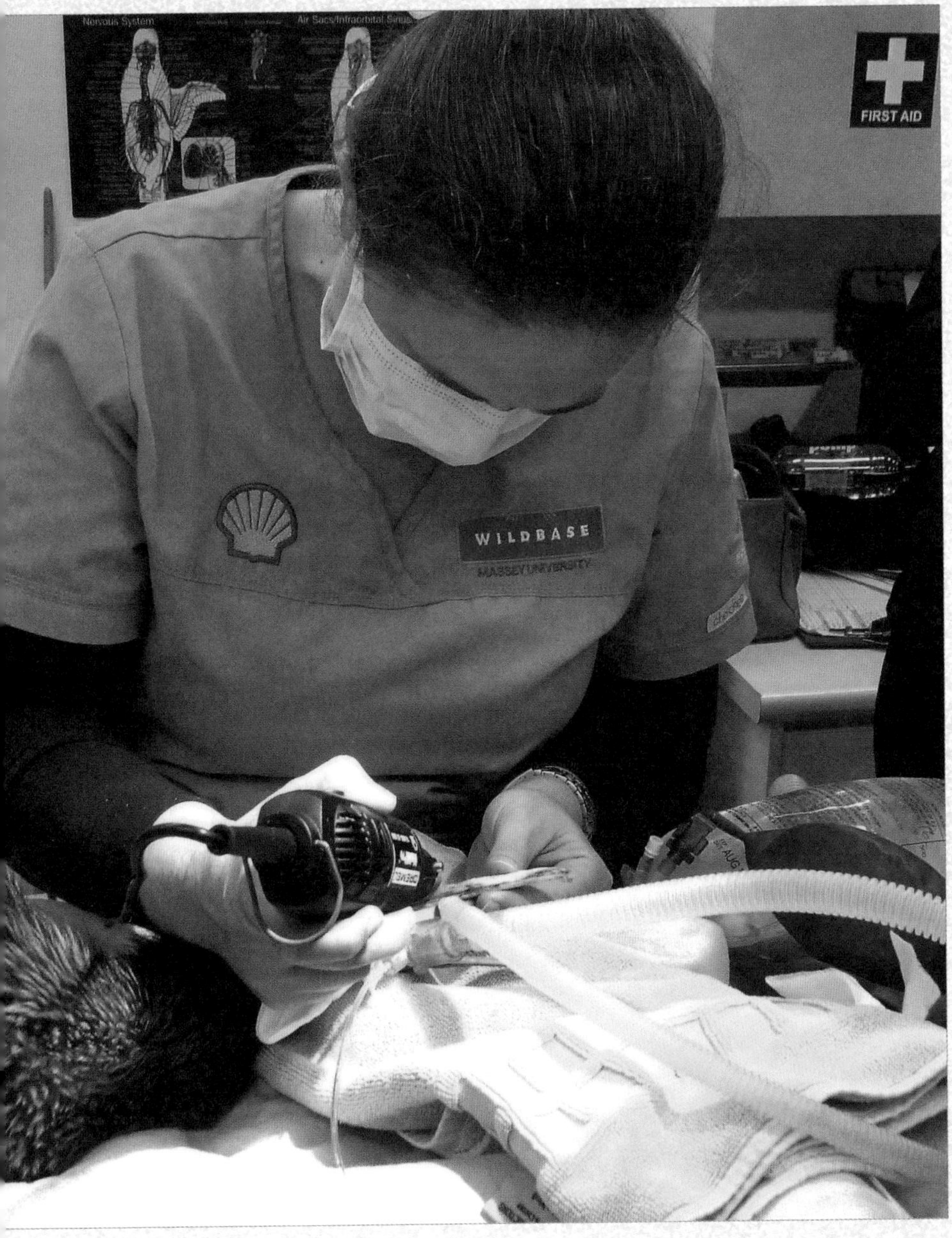

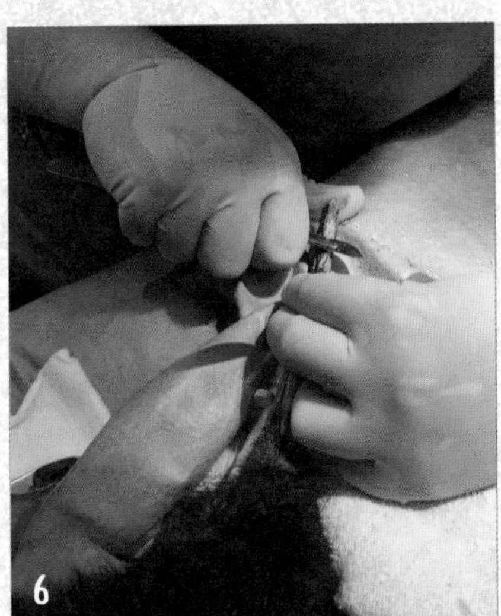

6

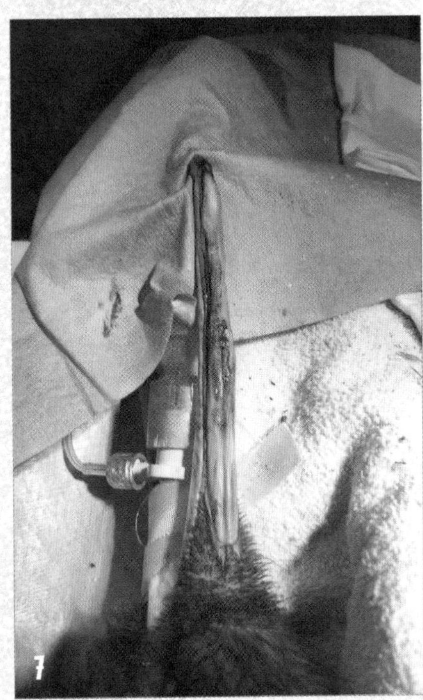

7

RARATOKA IS AT THE HOSPITAL for just over four months, but she is a challenging case. Wildbase has never had one quite like it before. How do you mend such a delicate instrument as a kiwi bill, especially when it must be used all the time for eating?

Megan coats the trimmed area with nail varnish to protect and strengthen it, but the varnish peels at the edges and an infection grows underneath. It's not working, and the bill is weakened and wobbly. The break must be held together and kept steady, but how can you do that? It's not possible to drill into the bill.

Bright idea!

Megan experiments with a technique that is sometimes used to mend turtle shells. Dress hooks are superglued on either side of the maxilla and rubber bands are looped in a figure-8 pattern to gently pull the break together. This is innovative, scary and exciting. It has never before been tried on a kiwi. *Will it work?*

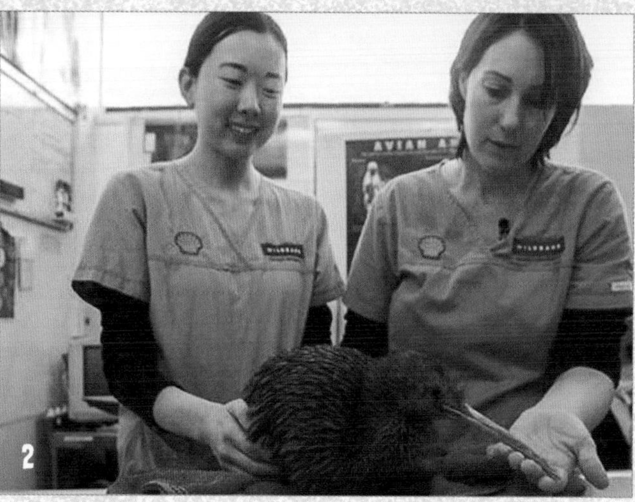

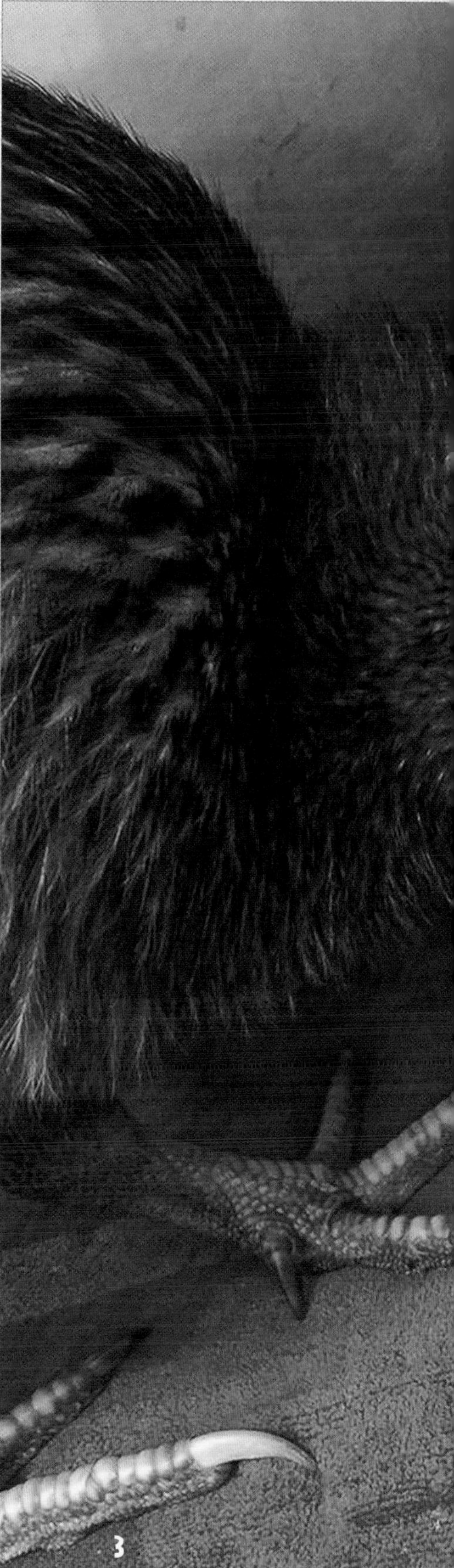

[1] Raratoka's varnished bill.

[2] Jamie (left) and Pauline with Raratoka.

[3] Raratoka probes the edge of her cage.

[4] The bill with its superglued dress hooks.

[5] A colourful array of rubber bands hold the bill exactly right.

[6] The X-ray with dress hooks clearly visible.

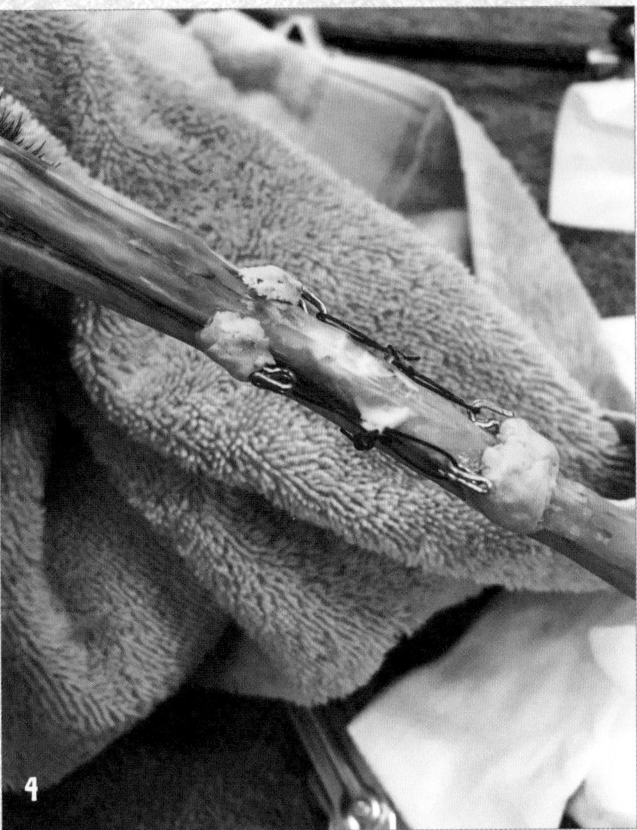
4

5

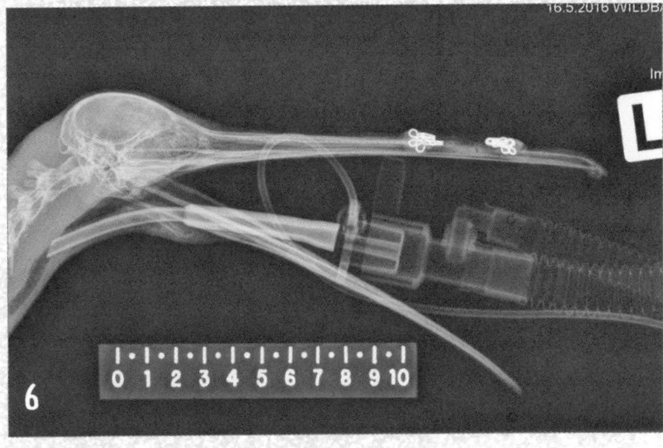
16.5.2016
L
0 1 2 3 4 5 6 7 8 9 10
6

BUT THERE'S A COMPLICATION. Caring for wildlife means not only mending bills or legs, flippers or wings: it also means managing behaviour . . . and Raratoka is *not happy!*

Tokoeka are famously grumpy. Because she can't eat as a kiwi usually does, she is force-fed — her bill is gently opened and food such as a mini meatball-for-kiwi is placed into her mouth where she can swallow it.

But she's not having that! She snorts and kicks and wriggles and struggles. She is stroppy. She doesn't like being handled; she doesn't want to be in hospital; she doesn't like dead food. She resists all the way.

SLOWLY, PATIENTLY, the Wildbase team nurses Rarotoka down the path to health. Days turn into weeks, and weeks become months. They keep Raratoka's pain levels down and encourage her to eat by herself. At the same time they keep the bill clean and healing. One nostril blocks. She has many general anaesthetics, many X-rays, many blood tests and surgeries. She still doesn't want to eat.

Her weight falls and falls, each day a little less. She must eat, but struggles so much when she is force-fed that the team has to give her liquid food by tube.

And at last she begins to turn around. Her bill heals and her weight increases. She is fed living things, such as earthworms and mealworms, and is moved from her cage into a larger space so she can move around and build up her appetite.

1

2

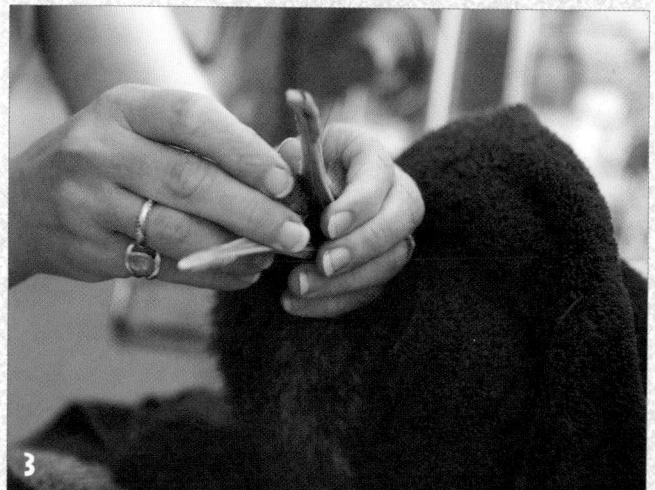
3

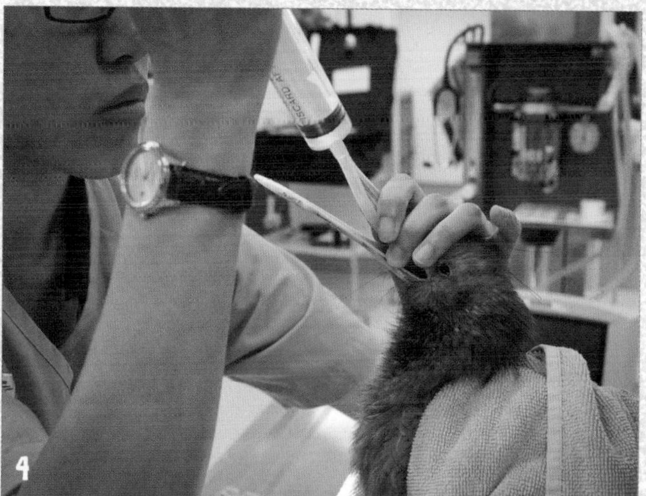
4

[1] One of Rarotoka's meatballs.

[2] and [3] Force-feeding meatballs to another kiwi with a damaged bill (not Raratoka).

[4] Tube-feeding the mince mixture after it has been ground into a fine slurry.

Raratoka is videoed at night, probing, eating and active.
The pretty pink bandage covers and protects a catheter on her leg. Catheters are thin tubes inserted into a vein and left in place. They are mainly used to deliver medicine.

AND NOW there's something else! All that sitting around doing nothing has turned Raratoka into a couch potato: she is incredibly unfit! She huffs and puffs at the least exertion and tires too quickly.

An ultrasound scan shows that her heart is slightly enlarged and beating too slowly. She needs to go to the gym!

Her fitness regime starts with little steps.

First, whenever she is put into her room, she is put further and further away from her house. She has to walk to go inside. She's put on a treadmill, but is stressed and frightened and is almost too tall for it anyway, so that stops.

Finally, almost miraculously, unbelievably, Raratoka is better. She's active at night. She's partying, eating by herself and biffing things around in her room. Her bill is as mended as it's ever going to be, and she is fit and ready to return to the south of the South.

RARATOKA DOESN'T GO BACK to the island. She is set free in the Haast Kiwi Sanctuary where her parents still live to this day. She is in a lovely bushy flat spot near the Arawhata River. Kiwi can live to 20 or 30 years. Hopefully she will pair up with her mate again and get on with the business of laying eggs and growing more tokoeka chicks.

PIWI'S TALE

1

PIWI IS A PUZZLE! Why is he so small? Why is he thin? Why isn't he growing? Why did he break his legs, first one, then the other? Is something seriously wrong with his bones?

There is a debate. Some think he should be euthanised. Others think he should be given a chance. Wildbase thinks so.

The path to Piwi's future is full of potholes and pitfalls, but along the way Piwi the puzzle becomes Piwi the pioneer.

2

LIKE LATITUDE, Piwi is a brown kiwi. His story begins in February 2008 in a burrow in Tongariro Forest Kiwi Sanctuary near Mount Ruapehu. He first comes to people's attention when DOC ranger Nicole checks him as a very new chick in the nest. He weighs 210 grams, which is rather small, but he is healthy. A chick-sized transmitter is attached to his right leg so he can be found again, and he is left to get on with feeding and growing by himself. He is checked now and then, and his transmitter is adjusted.

Eight months later, however, on Nicole's next visit, it is clear that things are not right. Piwi should weigh at least one kilogram but is only 437 grams — little more than a chick! He is tiny. He needs help.

He is transported to Rainbow Springs. A blood smear is taken and he is checked and microchipped. His right leg is sore from the transmitter, so a new one is put on his left leg. He is so thin you can see his backbone, and he has a small lump under his lower mandible, but the blood test is clear. The team at DOC and Rainbow Springs decide he should go to Warrenheip, where he can be more closely monitored.

Warrenheip is a large bushy valley that is kept safe from all kiwi-killing predators by a specially-designed fence (read more about it on page 39). Warrenheip is perfect for Piwi . . . but when he is picked up two years later, in December 2009, he is limping. At some time in those two years, he has broken the tibiotarsal bone in his right leg and it has healed badly.

Kiwi legs are right up there with kiwi bills for importance. They are strong and muscular and make up about a third of the bird's total body weight. Kiwi cover a lot of ground in one night, and can even run as fast as humans when they need to. They also use their legs for digging and fighting. Piwi can never prosper with his leg like this.

It's Wildbase for him!

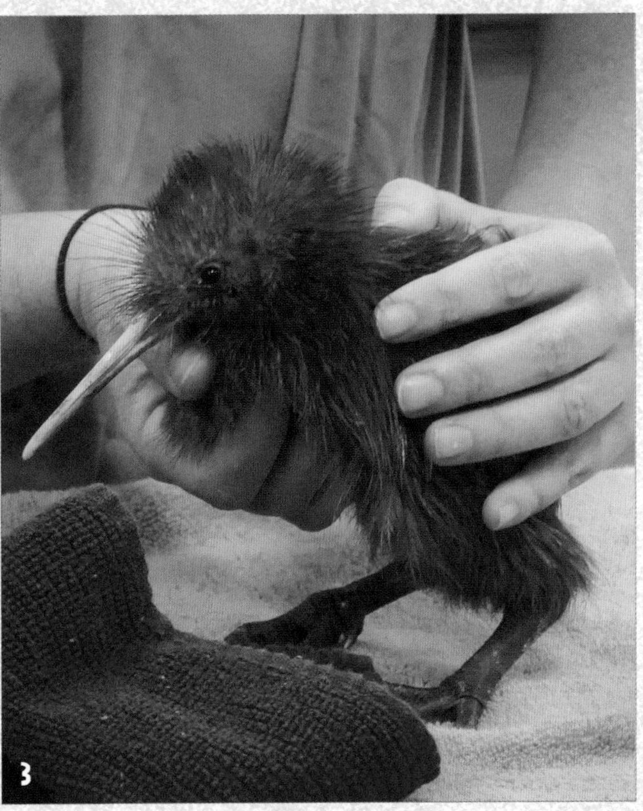

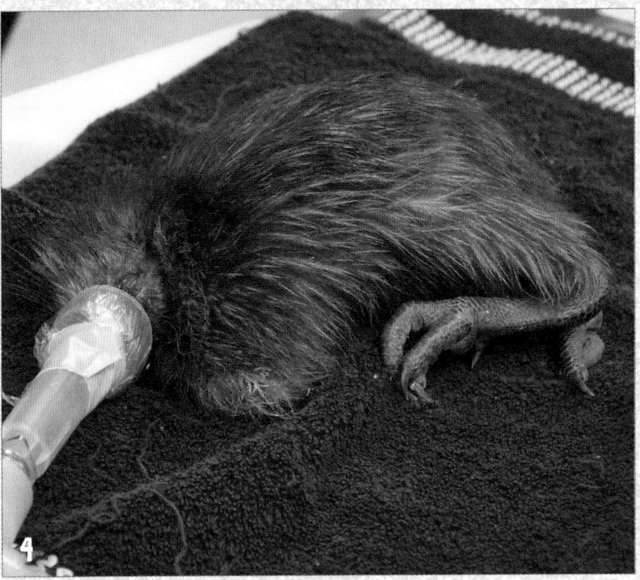

[1] A kiwi skeleton shows just how large the leg bones are compared with the rest of the bird.

[2] A young bird, just like Piwi.

[3] and **[4]** These photos are not of Piwi, because there are none of him from this time. Instead, this is another young brown kiwi, admitted to Wildbase Hospital suffering from hunger after a long, dry summer in the Hawke's Bay area. There are nearly always kiwi of all ages in the hospital, suffering from a wide range of illnesses and health problems.

PIWI GOES TO WILDBASE I

PIWI IS SMALL but he is young, and young bones heal more easily and more swiftly than older ones. On 9 December, Piwi is given a general anaesthetic, prepped for surgery and off he goes to the operating theatre. Brett, the vet, trims and rejoins the ends of his fractured leg bone. An external structure called a fixator holds the repair in place. It is routine surgery but there is a lot of bleeding. Piwi is given antibiotics and pain relief and taken to recover in a brooder.

Three days later, Piwi is bright, alert and hungry. By the end of the month, he is looking great. His leg is healing, he is gobbling his food and trashing his cage overnight. *That's always a great sign!*

But wait . . . it's too soon to celebrate. In January, Piwi is suddenly not hungry and his weight falls. Perhaps his leg is hurting? He is given more pain relief, X-rayed and double-checked. Nothing is obviously wrong.

On the first of February the fixator pins are removed, but Piwi is still unhappy and still not eating. He has to be force-fed. When he walks, he lifts his foot high and sometimes he knuckles over — his foot collapses under him. His right thigh muscles have weakened.

Piwi needs physio!

[1] The first X-ray, taken when Piwi was examined after he arrived in December, shows his broken right tibiotarsal bone.

[2] The second X-ray, taken in January, shows the repaired bone with the fixators holding everything steady.

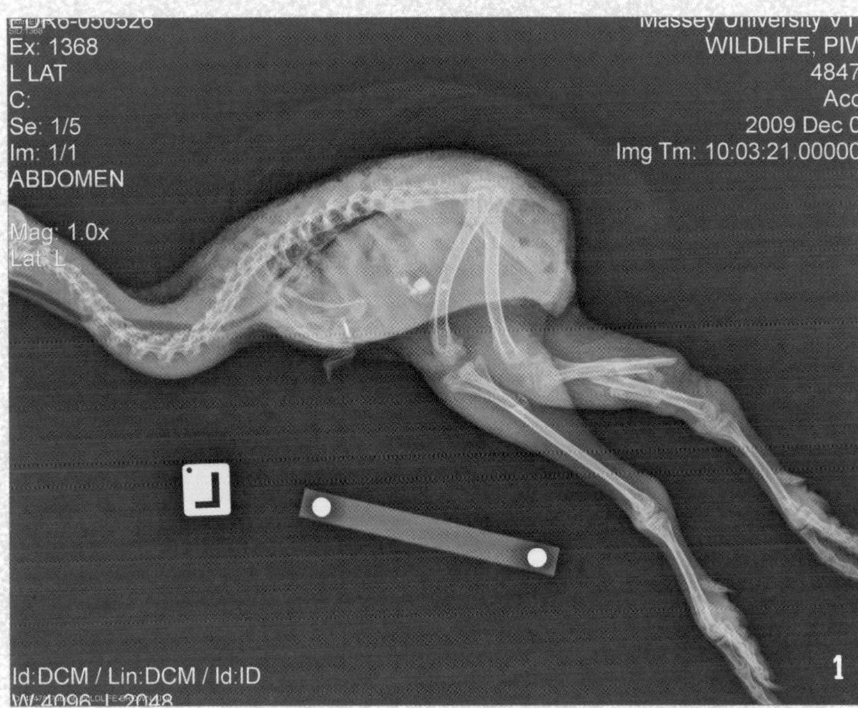

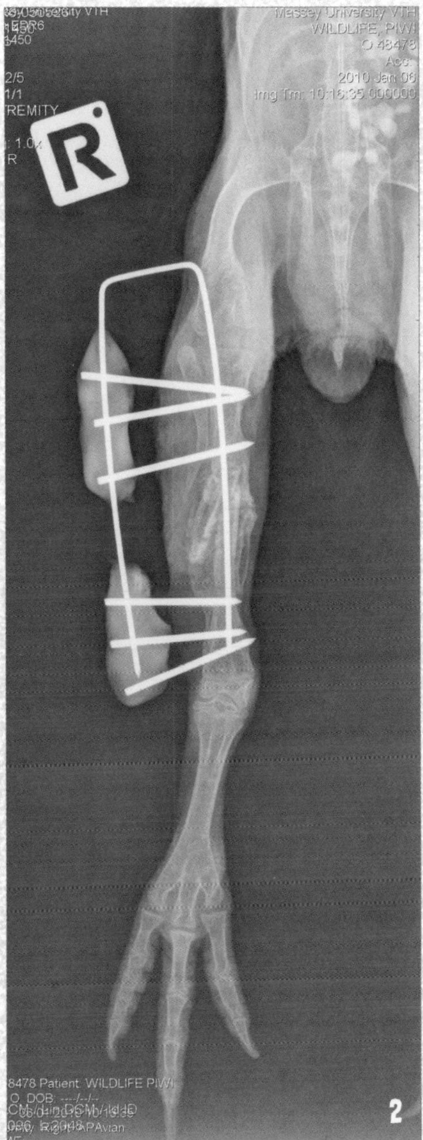

STEP-STEP-STEP. *Step-step-step.* It is like a nightmare. No matter how quickly he walks, no matter how hard he tries, Piwi is getting nowhere! He can't get to his little green house at the end of the runway.

Physio Fiona has prescribed treadmill workouts, massage and physio exercises, and he is on a treadmill that has been modified just for him. Dogs are sometimes put on treadmills to increase their fitness, but this is a first for a kiwi. Piwi is a pioneer! His story and a photo are in the Manawatū newspaper and he is on television.

Technician Pauline Nijman works with him. She and the other staff pull the sides along at precisely the right speed, keeping an eye on how he is going. Piwi has two 15-minute sessions a day. Each time, every day, he improves, slowly getting better.

BY THE END OF MARCH it is time to return to Rainbow Springs. Emma is looking forward to settling him in. He is going to start in a flat outdoor enclosure and gradually move to larger, more up-and-down spaces until he is ready to go back to the forest.

He is driven to Rotorua in a specially padded box and is fine when he arrives. Emma notes that his right leg is a little wasted but he is standing nicely. He is tucked in for the night in a brooder on special non-slip matting. ✔ *Tick! All is well!*

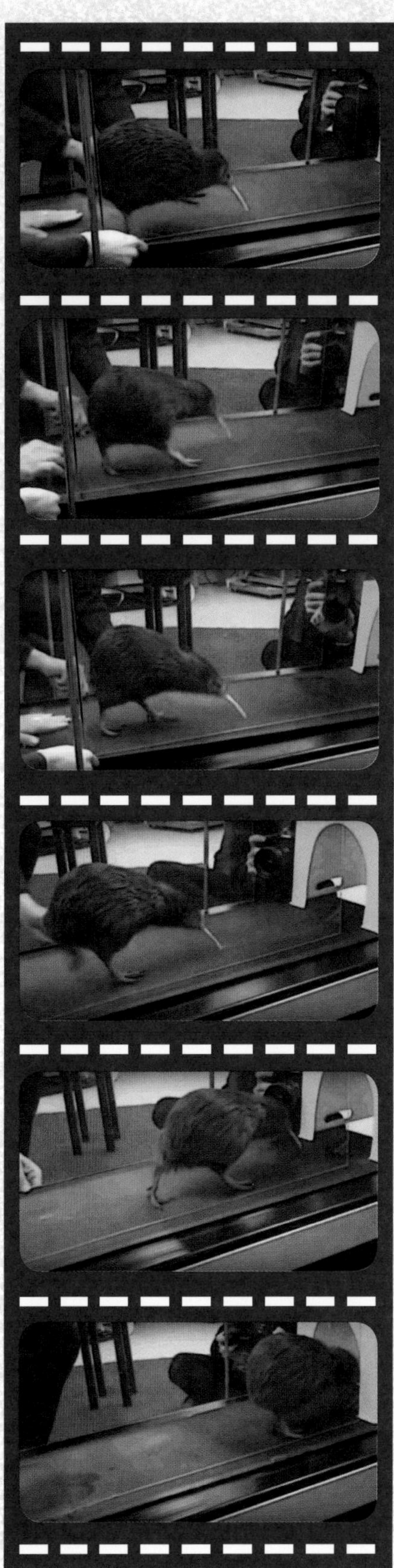

Step-step-step! Piwi is trying really hard to get to his little green house.

PIWI GOES TO WILDBASE II

EMMA AND BEV cannot believe what they see the next morning. It is dreadful. Piwi is flailing, staggering, thrashing about, trying to walk but falling helplessly, holding his left leg up.

He is rushed to the Rotorua vet. X-rays confirm what Emma already suspects: Piwi has broken his left femur. It's a bigger bone than the tibiotarsus and higher in the body. This break is more serious. Piwi is given pain relief and put on a plane back to Wildbase.

IT IS THE FIRST OF APRIL, but it is no joke for vets Brett and Lisa, who assess Piwi when he arrives. His right leg still looks all right, his bones check out OK, and they can see no reason not to try to mend the left leg. It is a bad break in three pieces, what is called a 'butterfly fracture'.

Piwi is taken to surgery. Coils of special cerclage wire hold the pieces together and, just as before, an external fixator supports the break.

The operation becomes more complicated when Piwi bleeds around the fracture before and during surgery, causing his blood pressure to fall. He is given 20 millilitres of blood from patient #49259, a recovering brown kiwi in the clinic.

Patient #49259 is also anaesthetised so blood can be taken from his jugular vein, and an anti-clotting agent is added before the blood is transfused into Piwi. At the same time Brett and Lisa give Piwi 90 millilitres of saline solution, antibiotics and a strong painkiller.

Back he goes, to intensive care.

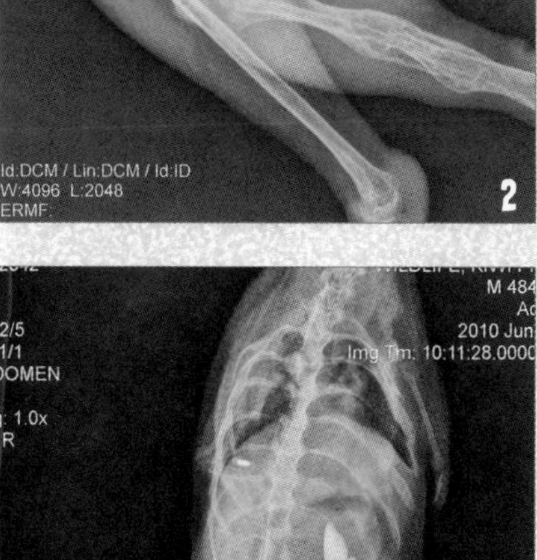

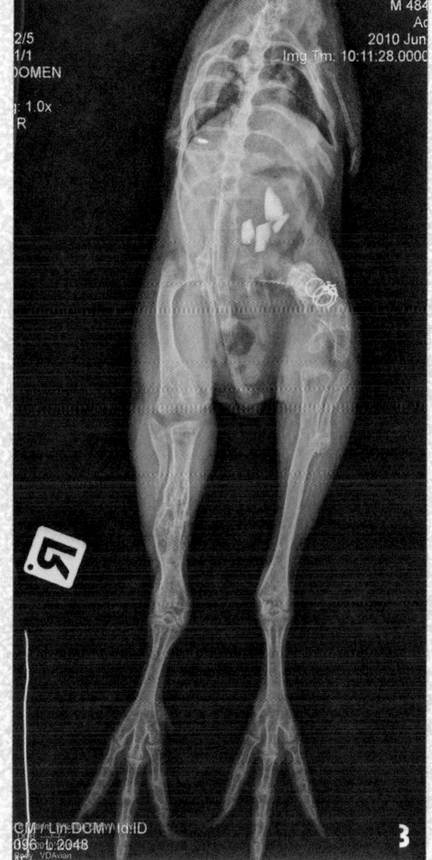

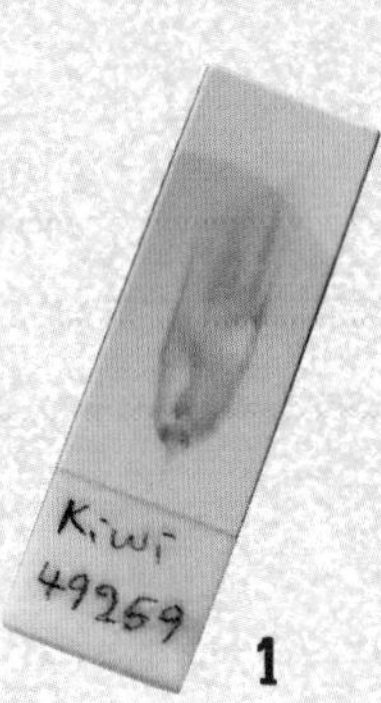

[1] Blood was taken from patient #49259 and transfused into Piwi after his blood pressure fell during surgery.

[2] This X-ray from 22 April shows the break in Piwi's femur and the fixator pins and cerclage wire holding the bones together. The small white shapes are stones in his gizzard, or stomach, that help him to break down and digest his food.

[3] This X-ray was taken on 11 June after the fixator was removed and healing was under way.

THEN COMES THE LONG, slow time when, day by day, step by step, Piwi gradually improves.

At first the team are happy that he can even stand without support.

But he has a setback; one morning, without warning, he seems uncomfortable. Something is hurting, but he can't tell Pauline what it is.

Perhaps he has knocked the fixator pin against the brooder walls? No one knows. He is given more pain relief, and it appears to help.

Then, just when things are looking up, Piwi develops osteomyelitis, an infection in the bone.

He is given different antibiotics plus calcium, and is treated under a UV lamp to increase his vitamin D levels and strengthen his bones.

On his first day under the lamp he lies back with his tummy exposed just like a person on a sunbed — *Oooh! That feels amazing!*

Through it all, though, the operation site is healthy and Piwi is able to walk in a limping kind of way. The fixator comes loose and is removed on 6 May. He continues to have a healthy appetite.

However, Piwi has been so long just sitting that his muscles and bones have become weak.

Back to the treadmill!

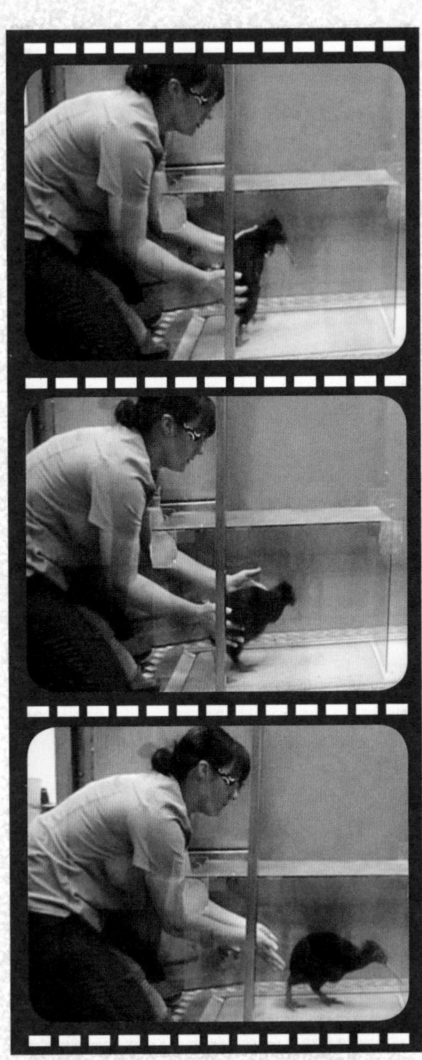

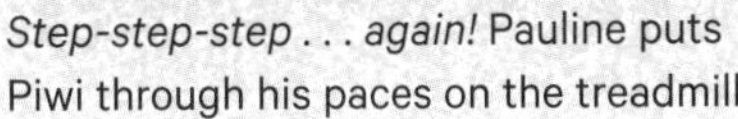

Step-step-step . . . again! Pauline puts Piwi through his paces on the treadmill.

At first, it is just gentle walking, but gradually the intensity increases. He has morning and afternoon sessions with Pauline on a special slow, quiet kiwi treadmill in a dark place. He's grumpy but, perhaps because he has been on one before, he tolerates it. He is walking with more strength than expected.

By June he is doing so well that he is moved to a larger room. It is reported that he has even been seen running! His back and leg muscles are bulking up: he is fitter and fitter — and because he is feeling like his old self, he is stroppier and stroppier! By July his limp is barely noticeable. His nails are trimmed. People begin talking about when he might be released.

ON 28 JULY Emma drives Piwi back to Rainbow Springs. For the first little while he is kept in two connected brooders. Everything goes swimmingly. He has peat moss to play in and is active at night, probing and filling his water bowl with dirt. He rolls a bit when he walks but he is still improving.

Piwi spends another two months at Rainbow Springs. His bill peels, which is alarming but actually no problem. Just as it was for Raratoka, because he had not been using the bill, the keratin has not worn down. He grows new feathers. He is moved to an outside enclosure. The forest is calling.

PIWI IS SET FREE in his old stomping ground, the forest of the Tongariro Kiwi Sanctuary, on 14 October. He doesn't have a transmitter because it would be too hard on his legs. We don't know how he's doing, but we like to think that somewhere out there, there's a smallish kiwi pottering, poking, sniffing, snorting and calling in the night. *Peewee! Peewee! Peewee!*

Off you go! Piwi returns to his old stomping ground, the forest of Tongariro Kiwi Sanctuary.

KEEPING PIWI SAFE

The Warrenheip Xcluder fence that protected Piwi from predators in his early years was developed in the 1990s and was the first of its kind in the country. The fence is high, with a curled top and with a foot buried in the ground. It is impossible for invaders such as stoats, cats, dogs and rats to dig under, climb, or jump over it. Most sanctuaries around the country, including the Central Energy Trust Wildbase Recovery Centre and Taranaki's Rotokare Scenic Reserve wildlife sanctuary (pictured), are kept secure by similar fences.

ABOUT WILDBASE

WILDBASE HOSPITAL

WILDBASE HOSPITAL is the main medical centre for New Zealand's sick and injured native birds, mammals and reptiles. It opened in 2002. Since 2017 it has operated from spacious new premises in the Institute of Veterinary, Animal and Biomedical Sciences at Massey University in Palmerston North.

In the hospital, at least two people always work with the patients, one a veterinarian and the other a technician. Because Wildbase is a training hospital, there are also student vets and techs watching and learning, preparing food, feeding the animals, giving medication, cleaning up and helping.

[1] Wildbase Hospital and ambulance.

[2] The Wildbase team on the day of Megan's graduation as a Master of Veterinary Science.

From left: Brett, director; Kat, veterinarian; Bex, rehabilitation technician; Megan, senior veterinarian; Jessica, veterinarian; Pauline, hospital and recovery supervisor; Alison, veterinarian.

Spot the photobomber!

THERE ARE TWO CATEGORIES of patients. The first are high priority because they are rare and endangered. Often, like Latitude and Raratoka, they are flown to Wildbase courtesy of Air New Zealand. They come from all over New Zealand, sometimes from as far away as Stewart Island, the subantarctic islands or the Chatham Islands.

They include land birds such as kea, kākā, kākāpō, kākāriki and takahē; water lovers such as matuku and whio; and seabirds like albatrosses, petrels and penguins. There are skinks, geckos and tuatara. And, of course, there are nearly always kiwi of all ages with a wide range of illnesses and health problems.

The second class of patients are the more common native creatures that we see in our everyday lives. They come from places closer to Palmerston North, from Manawatū, Taranaki and Hawke's Bay but no further.

This group includes birds such as gulls, tūī, piwakawaka, kererū, kōtare, pūkeko, tauhau/waxeye and kāhu/harrier hawk. And occasionally there are pets, such as turtles or bearded dragons, and tame or exotic birds like ducks and galahs.

They all sometimes need a hand!

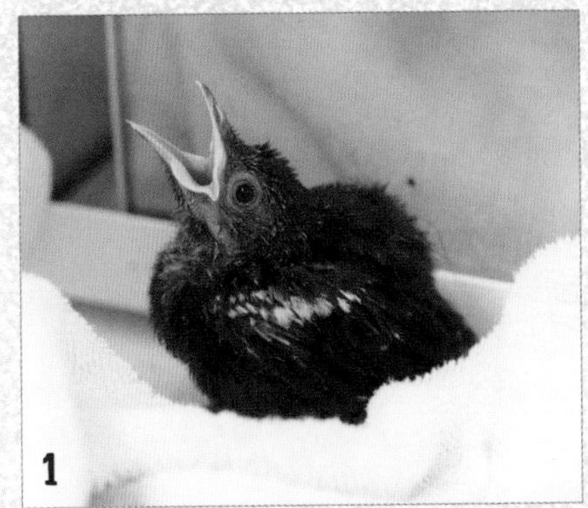

[1] This tūī fledgling fell from its nest and is being raised by Wildbase.

[2] A rare, endangered patient. The tuatara's distant ancestors lived in the same world as the dinosaurs. This character was weak and floppy when admitted, cause unknown.

[3] This river-loving whio, or blue duck, came to Wildbase looking sad and thin. By the time this photo was taken, it was ready to return to its river in Hawke's Bay.

[4] The white-faced heron, or matuku, is a common wetland-lover. This bird hurt its wing. It has been sedated and will soon be taken to surgery.

CENTRAL ENERGY TRUST WILDBASE RECOVERY CENTRE

WHAT HAPPENS WHEN a Wildbase Hospital patient has recovered from its medical emergency but is not quite ready for release to the wild? Sometimes, the animal will go back to the people who sent it to the hospital; sometimes it will go to a wildlife sanctuary or a bird rescue centre — but now there is another excellent option.

In early 2019 the Central Energy Trust Wildbase Recovery Centre opened for business. It is owned by the Palmerston North City Council and co-managed by the veterinary school. It is not far from Wildbase Hospital, and has been purpose-built so patients like Latitude and Piwi have somewhere to live while they recover their strength.

1

THERE ARE THREE MAIN PARTS to the centre. First, and most important, there's a zone with enclosures, pools and aviaries that are set aside for recovering patients. The public cannot go into this part, but they can peek through secret windows or watch videos of the animals as they move around.

It's all very high-tech — there are even cameras so the staff can check patients by remote control, without disturbing them.

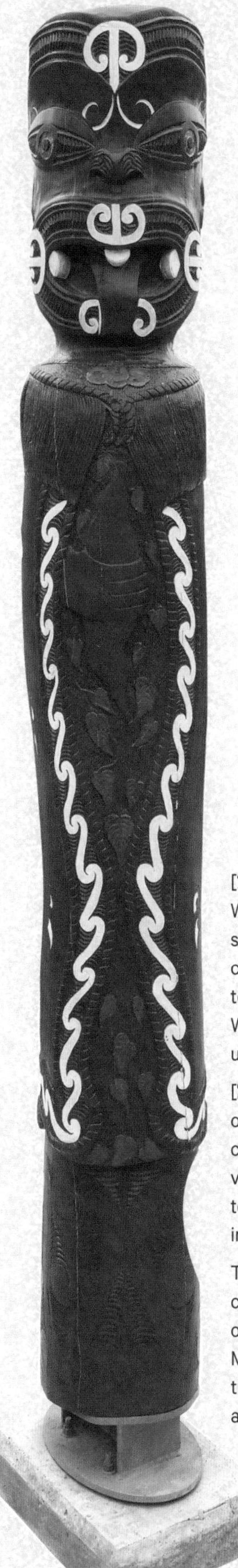

2

[1] The Central Energy Trust Wildbase Recovery Centre is secure behind predator-proof concrete walls with curled tops just like the ones around Warrenheip. The black poles hold up the nets for the aviaries.

[2] Rongo-mā-Tāne, the god of peace and agriculture. This ceremonial pou, or post, greets visitors just inside the entrance to the complex. It is one of many in the centre.

The pou remind us that the creatures inside are taonga, or precious treasures, to Māori. Mana whenua Rangitāne hold the kaitiakitanga role over native animals in Wildbase Recovery.

The public spaces include a courtyard, a walk-in aviary with birds such as tūī and korimako and a pool where you can watch rare pāteke.

Last but not least, there's a fabulous education centre where people can learn about the work of Wildbase and about New Zealand native wildlife. There's a resident teacher and lots of fun, informative and interactive displays and activities for children.

Visits to the centre are free, but it is not open to the public every day. Check the website before you go.

2

[1] Kāhu the harrier hawk is raring to go.

[2] The walk-in aviary.

[3] Kororā, or little penguin, in her own pool.

[4] Korimako, or bellbird, is one of the species in the walk-in aviary.

[5] Kārearea, the rare native falcon.

[6] What's inside this burrow?

[7] The education centre. *Very cool!*

[8] and [9] Oh, no! A kererū in trouble! Pauline is checking its pulse.

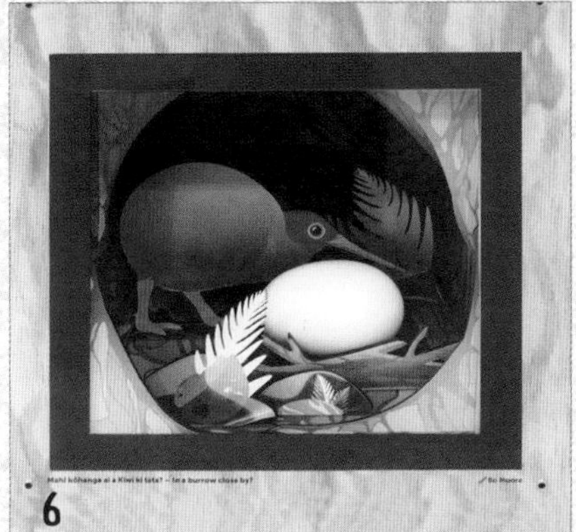

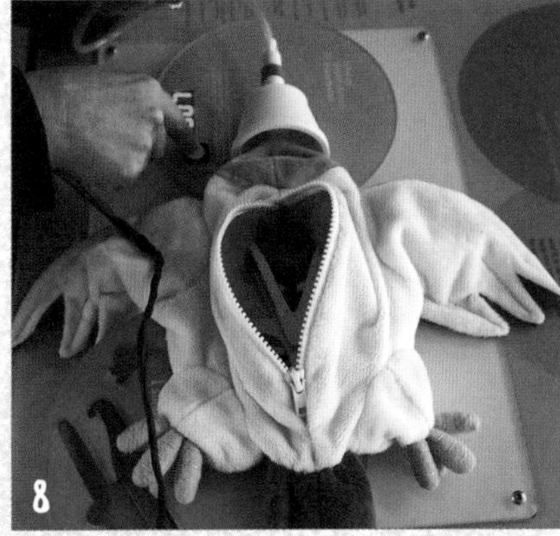

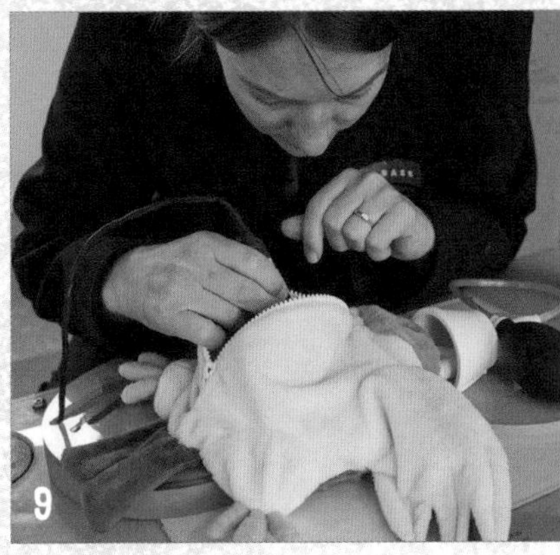

READING THREAT LEVELS

THE NEW ZEALAND THREAT CLASSIFICATION SYSTEM is a scale that tells us what shape our native animals are in. Scientists consider several different criteria when they assess the health of a species, and they are constantly reviewing and updating the lists. They ask:

1. *What is the population?* How many breeding adults are there? How large is the place where they live?
2. *What is the population trend?* Is it going up or down? How rapidly is this happening?

There are two categories, each with sub-sections.

THREATENED = In serious trouble and in great danger of dying out.

- A **NATIONALLY CRITICAL**: These species are at *immediate* risk of dying out.
- B **NATIONALLY ENDANGERED**:
- C **NATIONALLY VULNERABLE**:

} These also mean serious trouble but are not quite as dire as 'nationally critical'.

AT RISK = Not immediately likely to die out, but if their numbers continue to fall or a new threat arises, that could easily change. They are in trouble.

- A **DECLINING**: Numbers are falling, but still common.
- B **RECOVERING**: Numbers are low, but are now increasing after previously declining.
- C **RELICT**: Numbers are low but stable after previously declining.
- D **NATURALLY UNCOMMON**: A naturally small population that could easily become more endangered.

Read more at www.doc.govt.nz/nature/conservation-status.

EXTINCTION IS FOREVER

Since humans arrived in these islands around 800 years ago, 58 bird species and countless others have become extinct.

Like the piopio, a songbird that probably last lived in the same area of the North Island as Latitude and died out in the early 1900s, many of New Zealand's amazing creatures didn't stand a chance. It is thought that ship rats and stoats killed the last of them.

PIOPIO
LAST CONFIRMED SIGHTING: 1902

INDEX

WHERE ARE THEY NOW?

The wild is harsh and unforgiving. The best we can do is care for the environment, and when we can, provide second chances in places such as Wildbase Hospital.

Sadly, about a year after she was released, Raratoka's body was found. No one knows what happened or why she died.

Piwi has no transmitter, so his ultimate fate will never be known, but as far as we are aware he and Latitude are flourishing in their forests.

Go well! Keep safe!